The Last Fortress of Metaphysics

SUNY Series, Intersections: Philosophy and Critical Theory
───────────────
Rodolphe Gasché, editor

THE LAST FORTRESS OF METAPHYSICS

*Jacques Derrida and the
Deconstruction of Architecture*

Francesco Vitale
translated by Mauro Senatore

Cover photo of Tschumipaviljoen taken by Peter van Aller (from Groningen, The Netherlands). Retrieved from Wikimedia Commons.

Published by State University of New York Press, Albany

© 2018 State University of New York

All rights reserved

No part of this book may be used or reproduced in any manner whatsoever without written permission. No part of this book may be stored in a retrieval system or transmitted in any form or by any means including electronic, electrostatic, magnetic tape, mechanical, photocopying, recording, or otherwise without the prior permission in writing of the publisher.

For information, contact State University of New York Press,
Albany, NY
www.sunypress.edu

Production, Diane Ganeles
Marketing, Kate Seburyamo
Book design, Aimee Harrison

Library of Congress Cataloging-in-Publication Data

Names: Vitale, Francesco, 1971- author.
Title: The last fortress of metaphysics : Jacques Derrida and the deconstruction of architecture / by Francesco Vitale ; translated by Mauro Senatore.
Description: Albany, NY : State University of New York, 2018. | Series: SUNY series, Intersections: philosophy and critical theory | Originally written in Italian but not previously printed in Italy. First time in print. | Includes bibliographical references and index.
Identifiers: LCCN 2017023408 (print) | LCCN 2018011744 (ebook) | ISBN 9781438469379 (e-book) | ISBN 9781438469355 (hardcover) | ISBN 9781438469362 (paperback   )
Subjects: LCSH: Derrida, Jacques. | Architecture—Philosophy. | Deconstructivism (Architecture)
Classification: LCC B2430.D484 (ebook) | LCC B2430.D484 V5813 2018 (print) | DDC 194—dc23
LC record available at https://lccn.loc.gov/2017023408

10 9 8 7 6 5 4 3 2 1

CONTENTS

Acknowledgments vii

Introduction ix

Chapter One 1
The Law of the Oikos: *Jacques Derrida and the Deconstruction of the Dwelling*

Chapter Two 17
The House in Deconstruction: Notes on Derrida and the Law of the Oikos

Chapter Three 27
Jacques Derrida and the Politics of Architecture

Chapter Four 45
Mythographies: Toward an Architectural Writing

Chapter Five 63
Writing Space: Between Tschumi and Derrida

Chapter Six 79
Divergent Traces: Peter Eisenman as an Interpreter of Deconstruction

Chapter Seven 97
Spacing: The Architecture of Deconstruction

Notes 111

Bibliography 137

Name Index 145

ACKNOWLEDGMENTS

I MUST THANK RODOLPHE GASCHÉ NOT ONLY FOR WELcoming this book in his series but also for his teaching, which has accompanied me for years through the reading of Jacques Derrida, and above all for his friendship, which I consider the most precious of his gifts. I must also thank another master, the architect and theorist of architecture Vittorio Gregotti. I owe him the understanding of the (not only theoretical) stakes of the translation of deconstruction from philosophical writing to the theory and praxis of architecture. My thanks go also to Giovanna Borradori with whom I discussed almost every passage of this book; to Geoffrey Bennington for some essential remarks; to Peter Bojanic, who invited me to the conference Architecture of Deconstruction: The Specter of Jacques Derrida (Belgrade, 25–27 October 2012), thus giving me the opportunity to engage with architects and theorists of deconstructivism such as Eisenman, Tschumi, Kipnis, Cousin; to Francesco Rispoli, professor of architectural composition at the University Federico II, in Naples, who helped me deepen and test my architectural competencies; to Armando Sichenze, who invited me as a visiting professor to lead seminars on Architecture and Deconstruction at the Università della Basilicata, in Matera (Italy) from 2013 to 2015; to the architect Hosea Scelza, lifelong friend, who transferred to me the passion for architecture many years ago and with whom I designed the house where I live; to Andrea Canclini, Giovanni Durbiano, and Alessandro Armando, with whom I was able to discuss my theses on the relationship between deconstruction and deconstructivism, on the occasion of the lecture held at the Polytechnic University in Turin, in July 2015, and to Donald Cross, who helped me with proofreading. Finally, I thank Mme. Marguerite Derrida for allowing me to quote a few unedited texts from Derrida's archives at the IMEC, in Caen, and Bernard Tschumi for permission to use some pictures from his book *The Manhattan Transcripts*.

Derrida scholars will forgive me for simplifying the thought of the philosopher that I consider the master of masters. I believed it was necessary to make this work accessible to my friends who are architects and scholars of architecture. The latter will forgive me if, despite my best efforts, I haven't succeeded in my attempt at simplifying.

Some essays published in this volume originally appeared in Italian: "Introduction: The Last Fortress of Metaphysics" was included as the introduction to the volume in which I collected Derrida's writing on architecture, J. Derrida, *Adesso l'architettura*, a cura di F. Vitale (Milano: Scheiwiller, 2008); "The Law of the *Oikos*: Jacques Derrida and the Deconstruction of the Dwelling" develops the paper presented at the conference Architecture of Deconstruction: The Specter of Jacques Derrida (Belgrade, 25–27 October 2012); "Mythographies: Toward an Architectural Writing" and "Writing Space: Between Tschumi and Derrida" were published with different titles in my *Mitografie: Jacques Derrida e la scrittura dello spazio* (Milano: Mimesis, 2012); "Spacing: The Architecture of Deconstruction" appeared in *Annali della Fondazione Europea del Disegno (Fondation Adami)*, 2008/IV.

INTRODUCTION

THE INTEREST IN ARCHITECTURE CIRCUMSCRIBES A SPECIFIC moment of Jacques Derrida's work, at least at first glance: from "Labirinth und Architextur"[1] (1984) to "Talking about Writing"[2] (1993). This is a period of no more than ten years, in which Derrida is very active. He is among the promoters of the collaboration between the recently born Collège international de Philosophie and the Centre de création industrielle in Paris.[3] He writes a presentation for Bernard Tschumi's general project of the Parc de La Villette in Paris[4] and contributes to Peter Eisenman's project for a site in the park.[5] He gives a talk for the students of architecture at Columbia University and for avant-garde theorists such as Mark Wigley, Jeffrey Kipnis, and Anthony Vidler.[6] In 1991, he joins the Berlin Stadtforum, organized to discuss the future of the city after the fall of the Wall.[7] He takes part in the interdisciplinary symposium devoted to the Prague Urban Reconstruction project[8] and the presentation of Daniel Libeskind's project for the Berlin Jewish Museum.[9] He attends the first two meetings organized by Anyone Corporation, a team of architects and theorists created by Peter Eisenman and his wife Cynthia C. Davidson in the name of the architecture of the third millennium: in Los Angeles (1991) and in Yufuin in Japan (1992).[10] After 1993 this engagement with architecture ends. It was merely a break, a still in the film of a philosophical work that we can today designate as monumental. But it was enough for Derrida to be considered, whether rightly or wrongly, the founder of an architectural movement: so-called *deconstructivism*, which is more or less regularly identified with the work of the aforementioned Tschumi, Eisenman, and Libeskind, but also with Zaha Hadid, Rem Koolhaas, Coop Himmelb(l)au, Frank Gehry, and others.[11] To make the argument explicit, I begin by situating Derrida's work on architecture within a framework that clears confusing traces from the field of investigation and focuses on those traces that seem to be more pertinent for our investigation.

Each time unique. The encounter with architecture

Accidental and necessary at once: thus Derrida defines his encounter with architecture, namely, the relationship between deconstruction and architecture, according to a movement that is apparently contradictory and yet always at work in Derrida's writing, a movement that allows us to understand the general strategy underwriting his interventions on architecture as well as the singular character of each of them. We must take this movement into account; otherwise, we might run the risk of considering these interventions to be mere exercises of style, if not the occasional performances of a word magician—as Derrida still is for many readers. Indeed, it is not by chance that, declaring himself obstinately incompetent, Derrida recalls the surprise of that first time that inaugurated the series of subsequent encounters. Each time he goes back to the encounter with Tschumi and Eisenman and starts over. However, in so doing, he does not so much mean to gain the indulgence of his expert interlocutor as to shake a set of presuppositions that, remaining implicit, would affect the discourse about architecture, the relationship between architecture and deconstruction, according to a program that risks being taken as self-evident. Above all, Derrida does not mean to fall back into a classical philosophical position, which is rather to be contested: the absolute hierarchical privilege philosophy gives itself against the other fields of knowledge as the exclusive holder of the *true* discourse, the discourse all the other fields must refer to as the last instance. According to this schema, the philosopher to whom the architect appeals would be authorized to say the truth, the meaning, and destiny—the very essence—of architecture, which the architect is unable to grasp. The latter would be lost in his or her practice, which is always restricted even when strictly theoretical.

Although we are far from this tradition today, we still encounter this behavior, and not only in the field of architecture. Therefore, Derrida eludes the traditional form of the philosophical essay and prefers a direct confrontation, a discussion and exchange that are equal and take place in a public space, recognizable and shared. Indeed, he warns his interlocutors not to seek in his discourse a prescription valid for architecture and rather prefers to offer provocative and sometimes polemical observations. Furthermore, he does not give explicit definitions; he prefers raising questions to responding to them. Given the ironic tone and the elliptical form of his discourse, we may designate Derrida's position as *Socratic*. However, the goal is not to lead the interlocutor to the source of the truth that is present but forgotten in the soul, but to bring to light those traditional philosophical foundations that can (and cannot but) inhabit and govern, more or less secretly, the discourse and practice of architects, also of those architects who believe in their emancipation from tradition. However, contesting the privilege of philosophy does not mean setting the field free for different forms of competence, for instance, for the competence of architects with regard to problems related to architecture. Rather, it means challenging the very status of this so-called competence, generally speaking, and of architecture, in order to detect the necessity of a certain incompetence in the decisions that the architectural space demands. These decisions concern politics, economy, and culture but also the life of singular individuals, past, present, and future, who inhabit the architectural space. How do we establish a competence? Which institutions and institutional protocols grant it? Can we respond to the problems related to the architectural space by merely applying these competences? Do these problems not require the intervention of decisions that cannot be reduced to the order of an acquired competence? As the decisions the architect makes affect the space of the city in its complex articulations, internal and external, the architect must not only let other competences (political, economic, technical, etc.) intervene and negotiate with them. He also must respond to questions for which there is not nor could there ever be any competence. He must respond to the possibility of the to-come of the city and thus of the singular existences that inhabited, inhabit, and will inhabit it. By definition, the to-come cannot be anticipated by any calculation or program, and thus not by any competence. What is at stake here is the difficult question of responsibility, a question occasionally evoked in these interventions: a trace that Derrida follows throughout his path of investigation, which comes to the forefront in recent years and finds in the architectonic space an absolutely exemplary testing ground. On the one hand, the unexhausted complexity of conditions in which an architect must make a decision turns the latter into the witness of the irreducible aporia that every responsible decision must face by definition. On the other hand, this complexity allows us to grasp the immediately political character of any responsible decision, as it always concerns the relation to the other, every other, and above all to the alterity of the to-come. It is from this perspective that we must understand the question Derrida addresses to architecture: "Is an architecture of the event possible?"[12]

If the possibility of the to-come is the irreducible condition of our experience as well as of our existence, to make decisions concerning the to-come, while only holding on to already acquired competences, to an already given discourse, to the regulated and regular application established by this discourse, means to anticipate the to-come, to reduce it to the already known, and thus reduce, if not destroy, the possibilities that the to-come bears within itself in its irreducible randomness. To avoid reducing the encounter with architecture, the very relationship between deconstruction and architecture, to the simple application of a given, hierarchically organized program, Derrida insists each time on the surprise produced by this encounter and designates it as absolutely unexpected and unpredictable. In so doing, he also prevents deconstruction from the temptation of turning it into a new principle of reason, a new method or philosophical program that waits for its regular and regulated application in different fields of knowledge, thus neutralizing the possibility that each encounter might produce significant effects on both terms of the relationship instituted by the event. The event is an event as such only if it determines an absolutely new configuration with respect to the well-known premises that made it possible and, at the same time, achieves the redetermination of these premises that the event made somehow obsolete.

Always already at work. The deconstruction of architecture

However, the encounter between deconstruction and architecture is also necessary, even unavoidable. It is worth recalling briefly what the subject of deconstruction is. Derrida interrogates the philosophical tradition in order to understand why and how it has been constituted and generally imposed as "metaphysics of presence," according to Heidegger's definition; that is, as a thinking that thinks the being of beings according to the model of mere presence, in turn derived from the determination of the temporal present detached from the becoming that constitutes the irreducible element of our existence. Along this path opened up by Heidegger, Derrida operates a substantial detour, introducing the neologism *différance*, which allows him to focus on the dynamic character of difference as the irreducible condition of the possibility of presence and identity. Identity is not something *given* but is determined in relation to something else, in difference from itself, and, as such, it is not a stable, autonomous, and self-constituted presence. This differential relation underlies the determinate oppositions that constitute the field of metaphysics as their condition of possibility and as what those oppositions remove in order for the conceptual field to have its *conceptual consistency*. In particular, deconstruction allows us to determine that the oppositional determinations (culture/nature, history/technics, sensible/ideal, sign/signified, writing/thought, finite/infinite, etc.) that constitute the field of the "metaphysics of presence" are not simply specular but hierarchically organized. A term (or a group of reciprocally solidary terms) prevails over another term, namely, its opposite, in order to occlude, repress, remove, elude their irreducible relationship and thus the very possibility of a different elaboration of the conceptual field, an elaboration that would take into account the relation to the other as the condition of what is present and that thus has always already shaken and destabilized the constituted conceptual field. *Différance* can be forgotten or removed but precisely for this reason (because it cannot be simply destroyed, as a condition of possibility) keeps on producing uncanny effects on the system that is organized on the basis of its removal, and on related practices.[13] The "metaphysics of presence" is not a mere intellectual abstraction but the order of discourse that innervates the institutions governing our life, and thus also architecture—perhaps, architecture above all. The latter constitutes for Derrida the most resistant and evident manifestation of the metaphysical order:

> On the one hand, this general architectonic *erases* or *exceeds* the sharp specificity of architecture; it is valid for other arts and regions of experience as well. On the other hand, architecture forms its most powerful metonymy; it gives it its most solid *consistency*, objective substance. By consistency, I do not mean only logical coherence, which implicates all dimensions of human experience in the same network: there is no work of architecture without interpretation, or even economic, religious, political, aesthetic, or philosophical decision. But by consistency I also mean duration, hardness, the monumental, mineral or ligneous subsistence, the hyletics of tradition.[14]

We may say that by its own nature architecture has always been bound to the (theological and political) axiomatic valorization of presence. But what is the nature of architecture? Is it possible to think of an architecture detached from the order of discourse imposed by a certain nature, according to a given, hierarchical order? Perhaps it is, so long as the foundation of the order imposed on architecture as its own nature has needed architecture itself. From the outset—*paradeigma* is the project of the architect, as well as the exemplification of the work of the demiurge in Plato's *Timaeus*—philosophy has recurred to the terminology and symbology of architectural construction in view of its very foundation and construction as *oikonomika*. This can be seen from the house as the metonym of the inside of the soul, of the subject, of one's being close to oneself (*chez soi*), of the proper, up to the Heideggerian "house of Being." Certainly, we may say that these are mere metaphorical, or even didactic and explicative, uses. However, the very concept of the metaphor is an intraphilosophical construction that, in order to work as such, presupposes assimilation to the architectonic and thus the distinction between the inside and the outside, the proper and the stranger, the ideal and its sensible translation.

For this reason, Derrida observes, "[t]here is no longer any reliance on the concept of metaphor here"[15] when we interpret the relationship between philosophy and architecture and, in particular, between deconstruction and architecture. The relationship between philosophy and architecture has been a relation of reciprocal implication "in the most essential of cohabitations."[16] We cannot rigorously establish the *proper* of the one with respect to the other nor, thus, their reciprocal transition and derivation.

Derrida has always been well aware of this point: from his first studies on Plato to his reinterpretation of the Freudian dynamic of the *Unheimlich*—the uncanny—a constant reference for the elaboration of the notion of a living human singularity on this side of any traditional determination of the subject, consciousness, and ipseity in general. From this perspective, the deconstruction of architecture has always already been at work through the deconstruction of philosophy.[17] However, thanks to architects, and in particular to the work of Eisenman, Derrida realizes that the encounter with architecture is absolutely necessary for deconstruction. There is no effective deconstruction if the latter is unable to intervene in architecture, to win out over the theoretical, political, institutional, symbolical, and material resistances that turn it into "the last fortress of metaphysics."[18] Deconstruction must be able to turn itself into a work, materialize in the symbolical and institutional space occupied by architecture:

> A consistent deconstruction would be nothing if it did not take account of this resistance and this transference; it would do little if it did not take on architecture as much as the architectonic. To take it on: not in order to attack, destroy, or lead it astray, to criticize or disqualify it. Rather, in order to *think* it in fact, to take sufficient distance from it so as to apprehend it in a thought that carries beyond the theorem—and becomes an oeuvre in turn.[19]

Deconstruction has always already been at work, independently from anyone's will, it inhabits as a ghost the architecture of Western thought and its well-structured tradition. Deconstruction as an explicit theoretical discourse is only a local symptom—the philosophical space—of the impossible removal that grounds this general architecture and allows the latter to impose itself pervasively. This means that deconstruction cannot but shake architecture as a different articulation of the same tradition. But the work of desedimenting and uncovering must necessarily take place from within architecture and thus with help from architects who had found in deconstruction useful tools for putting the inherited tradition into question, in their field and according to its specificity. The work of those who intend to focus on the effects of deconstruction in a determinate field does not intervene from outside, does not apply a rule produced somewhere else with respect to the inhabited architecture, but visits the latter's places, uses its resources, knows its most remote corners and thus can detect the inconsistencies and points of rupture of that specific structure. Each time deconstruction is a singular experience and thus must be left to its essential drift, through which, each time, it changes and rewrites itself, thanks to someone involved in it, even if this implies a radical transformation of sense. Derrida never opposes a right of exclusive property to this movement of contamination and dispersion and yet always appeals to a certain vigilance, if not in defense of deconstruction, at least to defend himself from assimilations he considered unproductive if not unfair, such as "the postmodern" or "nihilism,"[20] as well as from a certain use of deconstruction made by architects. In particular, I refer to the cases in which the discourse of architects risks falling back into the metaphysics of presence they aim to contest. This is the case of Eisenman, often invited by Derrida to account for the use of a precise locution—"the presence of an absence"—as the theoretical mover of his work.

Which architecture? The architecture of deconstruction

Therefore, the deconstruction of architecture has been at work since the beginning. But in view of what? Is it possible to say? Can we detect the effects of such an encounter on both architecture and deconstruction? I limit myself to describing two trajectories that I think should be followed: on the one hand, we must dissociate architecture from those ends it has been submitted to throughout its history: religious, political, economic, aesthetic, social purposes as well as the purposes of Heideggerian "inhabiting." According to Derrida, these purposes neither define the essence of architecture nor exhaust the horizon of its possibilities; perhaps they reduce it by removing its irreducible potential. Furthermore, these purposes are intimately solidary with one another, an expression of the same, unique purpose, the purpose of the metaphysics of presence:

> *Architecture must have a meaning*, it must *present* this meaning, and hence *signify*. The signifying or symbolic value of this meaning must command the structure and syntax, the form and function of architecture. It must command it *from the outside*, according to a principle (*archē*), a grounding or foundation, a transcendence or finality (*telos*) whose locations are not themselves architectural.[21]

Therefore, we must neither reconstitute a supposed original purity of architecture, nor carry out a meaningless architecture without ends and functions. Rather, we must call into question the subordination and integration of architecture within a given understanding of the production of sense, an understanding that seems obvious and natural but is proper to the order of the metaphysics of presence—that is, it is historically determinate. This understanding presupposes the autonomy of the production of meaning with respect to the means that it subordinates to its transmission and sharing, and thus it excludes the possibility that transmission and sharing constitute on the contrary the ultimate conditions of the production of sense. This is the possibility we must interrogate in architecture, but not only from a theoretical and critical perspective. For Derrida, architecture should construct by deconstructing the paradigm of finalities in all its articulations, by taking up deconstruction as its theoretical as well as practical and constructive matrix. How should architecture do this? By highlighting and reinscribing the functions that traditionally govern architecture within a broader construction, which would be articulated differently and no longer subordinated to these functions. It is from this perspective that Derrida is interested in the productive contamination of languages and writings, in the use of procedures imported from musical or cinematographic works (see the works of Libeskind and Tschumi), in the recourse to literary forms and figures (see the case of Eisenman).

On the other hand, through the same upstream movement toward the conditions of possibility, we must think architecture in terms of writing, according to the extension and profundity Derrida attributes to this notion (renamed *arche-writing*). For Derrida, it is necessary to go back to this term to describe the conditions of possibility of experience: there is an experience—even the most intimate and secret one—only when we register its inscription at the level of an iterability to come in a space that is already the space of our consciousness and that is constituted as such only thanks to this inscription, opening to alterity in general. This spacing has always already been at work before any effective spatial experience that the tradition has taught us to consider secondary and external with respect to a consciousness that has already been constituted as such in the intimacy of a self-presence independent from any reference to the other. Thanks to this irreducible spacing, consciousness has already been open and is in a relationship with alterity in general: it has already been involved in the becoming space of experience. It is to this point that Derrida seems to refer when he defines architecture as "writing of space,"[22] not only as the objective articulation of singular experience, according to its several stratifications (from individual desire to the most general being-with-others) but, above all, as the condition of the taking place of experience, of the invention of the place where something like sense can happen, being transmitted and shared. Through this movement, architecture takes up the most urgent responsibility, that of giving place to the possibility of the to-come, of becoming a work, an institution, a trace of ink or stone, or of something else, in order for something else to happen.

I

THE LAW OF THE *OIKOS*

*Jacques Derrida and the
Deconstruction of the Dwelling*

DERRIDA'S CONCERN FOR ARCHITECTURE IS JUSTIFIED BY the specific question of dwelling. As I aim to demonstrate, this question is at the very origin of deconstruction and, ultimately, the deconstruction of architecture is a necessary moment of deconstruction itself. To this extent, quoting Derrida from "No (Point of) Madness—Maintaining Architecture," I recall that "[a] consistent deconstruction . . . would do little if it did not take on architecture."[1] Then, Derrida argues that architecture is "the last fortress of metaphysics."[2] However, he also says that what we consider the essence and sense of architecture is indeed the legacy of a specific, historical determination:

> Let us not forget that there is an architecture of architecture. Down to its archaic foundation, the most fundamental concept of architecture has been *constructed*. This naturalized architecture is bequeathed to us: we inhabit it, it inhabits us, we think it is destined for habitation, and it is no longer an object for us at all. But we must recognize there an *artifact, a constructum*, a monument. It did not fall from the sky; it is not natural, even if it informs a specific scheme of relations to *physis*, the sky, the earth, the mortal, and the divine. This architecture of architecture has a history; it is historical through and through. Its heritage inaugurates the intimacy of our economy,

the law of our hearth (*oikos*), our familial, religious, and political oikonomy, all the places of birth and death, temple, school, stadium, agora, square, sepulcher. It penetrates us [*nous transit*] to the point that we forget its very historicity: we take it for nature. It is good sense itself.[3]

Therefore, architecture is not merely "the last fortress of metaphysics" as such, by essence or necessity. It has become what it is when submitted to a specific law of dwelling:

> The experience of meaning must be the *dwelling* [habitation], the law of the *oikos*, the economy of men or gods. . . . The arrangement, occupation, and investment of locations should be measured against this economy. . . . Centered and hierarchized, the architectural organization will have had to fall in line with the anamnesis of its origin and the basis of a foundation. Not only from the time of its founding on the ground of the earth, but also since its juridico-political founding, the institution that commemorates the myths of the city, the heroes or founding gods. Despite appearances, this religious or political memory, this historicism, has not deserted modern architecture. Modern architecture is still nostalgic for it: it is its destiny to be a guardian. An always hierarchizing nostalgia: architecture will have materialized this hierarchy in stone or wood (*hylē*); *it* is a hyletics of the sacred (*hieros*) and the principle (*archē*), an *archihieratics*.[4]

Here Derrida refers to a specific law of dwelling, which is historically determined: the law of the Greek *oikos*. A law that is rooted in an archaic or mythico-religious experience of space and place, which is so powerful as to govern still the distribution of spaces and places that identify individuals and a community with a certain territory. In order to grasp the bearings of that law, it is worth remarking that, for Derrida, it does not work only for architecture; yet, all aspects of our culture and thus of philosophy are subjected to this law. The reason why architecture is so important for Derrida is that

> [o]n the other hand, architecture forms its most powerful metonymy; it gives it its most solid *consistency*, objective substance. By consistency, I do not mean only logical coherence, which implicates all dimensions of human experience in the same network: there is no work of architecture without interpretation, or even economic, religious political, aesthetic, or philosophical decision. But by consistency I also mean duration, hardness, the monumental, mineral or ligneous subsistence, the hyletics of tradition. Hence the *resistance*. the resistance of materials like the resistance of consciousness and unconsciousness that establishes this architecture as the last fortress of metaphysics.[5]

Deconstructing architecture means, therefore, deconstructing the law of the *oikos* that determines the essence of architecture in our tradition, as well as realizing the most general aim of deconstruction. It is from this perspective, I argue, that Derrida proposes to Peter Eisenman to start their collaboration through a reading of Plato's *Timaeus* and of his commentary on this work. The reference is to *Khōra*.[6] The choice of *Timaeus* is evidently accurate: this is one of the foundational texts of the philosophical as well as of the architectural tradition (in particular, of one of the latter's highest moments, the Renaissance). In the *Timaeus* we find the metaphor of the demiurge as "divine architect" who brings the ideal into the sensible through calculation and geometry. But we also find a paradigmatic analogy between the human body and the structure of a building and a city, an analogy that goes back to the medical school of Cos, which, through Plato, imposes the law of central and hierarchized symmetry to the construction of discourse as well as to sculpture and architecture. More generally, it is in the *Timaeus* that the question of *khōra* establishes the coordinates of Western speculation on space, from Aristotle's criticism up to the Cartesian notion of space as the condition of the *res extensa* and thus to Heidegger, who sees Plato's *khōra* at the origin of the metaphysical determination of space.[7] For this reason, Heidegger deemed it necessary to go back to the originary Greek conception of dwelling in order to gain an experience of space that would be nonmetaphysical and to start from there a reconsideration of dwelling itself. In my view, Derrida suggests a return to *khōra* in order to acknowledge that both philosophy and architecture have been submitted to the archaic law of dwelling, the law we must not go back to, as Heidegger suggested, but which we must deconstruct and conjure away, in view of another dwelling, a dwelling to come. In "No (point of) Madness—Maintaining Architecture," Derrida precisely demarcates his position from that of Heidegger on the question of the law of the *oikos*:

> Heidegger still alludes to it when he interprets homelessness (*Heimatlosigkeit*) as the symptom of ontotheology and, more precisely, of modern technology. . . . This is not a deconstruction, but rather a call to repeat the very fundamentals of the architecture that we inhabit, that we should learn again how to inhabit, the origin of its meaning.[8]

Before returning to *Khōra*, I want to remark that Derrida began to deal with the law of the *oikos* much earlier than the time at which he began to meet architects. We may reframe the whole path of deconstruction in the wake of this question. This is particularly evident in "Plato's Pharmacy," which ends up announcing the work on *khōra* Derrida will complete twenty years later. First, Derrida makes a bold and, in my view, important point: the system of conceptual opposition that constitutes Platonic metaphysics rests on a nonconceptual opposition, which Plato himself does not develop in conceptual terms, as it cannot be done:

> In order for these contrary values (good/evil, true/false, essence/appearance, inside/outside, etc.) to be in opposition, each of the terms must be simply *external* to the other, which means that one of these oppositions (the opposition between inside and outside) must be already accredited as the matrix of all possible opposition. And one of the elements of the system (or of the series) must also stand as the very possibility of systematic or seriality in general.[9]

At the foundations of the system of metaphysics there is a spatial opposition, the inside/outside opposition, which is not purely conceptual but sensible, empirical, coming from an ordinary experience that appears obvious to Plato himself. According to Derrida, we can find the testimony of this experience of space in the archaic rituals of purification of the city, which survive in the *polis* of the classic age. Derrida writes:

> The Character of the *Pharmakos* has been compared to a scapegoat. The *evil* and the *outside*, the expulsion of the evil, its exclusion out of the body (and out) of the city—these are the two major senses of the character and of the ritual. . . . The city's body *proper* thus reconstitutes its unity, closes around the security of its inner courts, gives back to itself the word that links it with itself within the confines of the agora, by violently excluding from its territory the representative of an external threat or aggression. That representative represents the otherness of the evil that comes to affect or infect the inside by unpredictably breaking into it. Yet the representative of the outside

is nonetheless *constituted*, regularly granted its place by the community, chosen, kept, fed, in the very heart of the inside. . . . The ceremony of the *pharmakos* is thus played out on the boundary line between inside and outside, which it has as its function ceaselessly to trace and retrace. *Intra muros/extra muros*.[10]

This is the origin of the law of the *oikos*: the mythico-religious experience that still survives in the organization of the space of the *polis*, and, at the same time, constitutes the paradigm of ontological identity understood as a permanent and stable presence, independent and autonomous from the alterity to which it is detached as the inside from the outside. But it is necessary to return to Khōra to understand the phantasmatic ground (which is powerful as much as it is illusory), that, according to Derrida, still haunts our dwelling. At least this is the hypothesis I will test in the next section.

Politics of Khōra

In order to grasp the political dimension of the *Timaeus* and of the ontological question posed in *Khōra*, it is necessary to refer to other texts by Derrida, which are still unpublished and which I had the opportunity to read in the Derrida archives. In particular, I refer to a seminar of 1985–1986 entitled "Nationalité et nationalisme philosophique: mythos, logos, topos," whose first six sessions focus on the *Timaeus* and the question of *khōra*.[11] In fact the text proposed to Eisenman is a quite bizarre editing of excerpts from this seminar. Here we can see that the stakes of Derrida's reading are political. In fact, the *Timaeus* continues a dialogue that took place the day before, where Socrates described "the ideal polis and its constitution,"[12] and that can be identified with the *Republic*. From the first conversation, we know that the dialogues take place during the Pan-Athenian celebrations, which had the character of a national celebration and involved the entire population. The celebration is devoted to Athena, the goddess, founder and protector of the city. A spectacular procession used to climb the Acropolis up to the temple of Athena where an impressive sacrifice celebrated the divine origin of the city and renewed the alliance with the protector goddess. The core of the cult was the myth of the autochthony of the Athenians' ethnicity, that is, the myth of Erichthonius, who was born directly from earth, not from a woman, but from the soil fecundated by the seed of Hephaestus, dispersed after his clumsy attempt to possess Athena. At the top of the Acropolis, in the archaic age, the Erecteion was the oldest temple and was dedicated to these myths of foundation and thus also to the cult of Erichthonius, the king-God of the origins. When in the classical age it was rebuilt in another place, the original foundations were retained. Therefore, during the Pan-Athenian celebrations, the people of Athens, the sons of the earth, celebrated at the same time the divine and autochthonous origin of their *genos*, which made them exceptional and superior with respect to the other Greeks.[13] As it is well known, first Cimon and then Pericles invested huge amounts of capital to rebuild the Acropolis after its destruction by the Persians, in order to restore its symbolic value and thus to remove the trauma inflicted on Athenian identity by the foreign invasion. The most important architects of the age were involved in the work of reconstruction, which can be seen as a paradigm of Western architecture. The whole architectural organization seems structured according to that symbolic project, which found in the Pan-Athenian celebrations its concrete and spectacular realization. In particular, in the processional ascension we find represented a divine procession in the extraordinary, internal frieze of the Parthenon, realized by Phidias and his disciples.[14] In the seminar devoted to the *Timaeus*, Derrida lingers on this celebration, on its spatial organization and its archaic cause, at the roots of the myth of autochthony. In particular, he focuses on the itinerary of the procession along the sacred way. The procession leaves from the lower city, namely, the Ceramic, where the famous Athenians are buried, passes by the agora, the secularized space of the political, goes up to the Acropolis, and ends before the impressive statue of Athena. The following remark by Derrida is the key to understanding what is at stake here: "At the Ceramic, in the civic ground (*khōra*) they come from, the sons of the polis are buried: time annihilates through the return of the end to the origin."[15]

I emphasize the word between parentheses: the civic ground is called *khōra*. We should read the *Timaeus* from this perspective. This is the subject of the dialogue: sketching out, along with the *Critias*, which was never finished, and, perhaps, with the *Hermocrates*, which was never written, the complete table that would make possible the transition into historical reality of the perfect city Socrates described according to its ideal traits in the *Republic* and, briefly, at the beginning of the *Timaeus*. This general table responds to an urgent political necessity: Timaeus and Critias must expose the possibility of putting the ideal *polis* into action in historical becoming, the possibility of the passage from the ideal to the sensible. This possibility must be grounded on the origin and structure of the universe and, thus, on the origin and history of the city that is supposed to actualize it, namely, Athens. Socrates himself delineates in these terms the order of the dialogue and the tasks of the interlocutors: Timaeus performs the onto-cosmological reconstruction, from the origin of the universe to the anthropological structure of man, while Critias reconstructs the origin of the people of Athens and their history. Therefore, Plato aims to demonstrate the congruity of his ideal and political construction with the ontological foundations of all that is, and thus the possibility of the concrete actualization of the ideal in a specific place (Athens). But we can also suppose that the ontological, cosmological, and anthropological determinations are constructed so as to resonate with the possibility of the actualization of the ideal polis. Let me follow the initial lines of the *Timaeus* up to the point when Socrates assigns Timaeus and Critias the task of making the ideal polis sensible. He has just summarized the essential passages of the discourse held the day before on "the city—*politeia*—and its constitution." Hence, Socrates lets his interlocutors speak: he described the essence of the perfect *polis*, but this is only a fixed, motionless, and lifeless image (*hypo graphés*). It is time to make it lively, to bring it from essence to existence. This passage is decisive: the essence of *polis* takes its life in war. War is the proof against which one must measure the possible actualization of the political ideal:

> I should like to hear an account of it putting forth its strength in such contests as a State will engage in against others, going to war in a manner worthy of, and achieving results befitting, the training and education given to its citizens, both in fears of arms and in negotiation with various other States.[16]

War and thus the affirmation and defense of one's identity against the identity of others: this is the goal of the ideal construction of the *polis* and, therefore, the ground on which the very constitution of the *polis* lies and organizes itself. Derrida writes:

> To give birth—but this is also war. And therefore death. This desire is also political. How would one animate this representation of the political? . . . The possibility of war makes the graphic image (*hypo graphés*)—the description—of the ideal city go out, not yet into the living and mobile real, but into a better image, a living image of this living and mobile real, while *yet* showing a functioning that is internal to the test: war. In all the senses of the word, it is a *decisive exposition* of the city.[17]

The ideal determination of the city must be tested through its existence, and this existence, the life of the ideal city, consists in war. Its relationship with other cities is thought in terms of conflicting opposition. The other as such is stranger and foreign, a threat for the life of the city, which is conceived as an interiority faced with a certain outside. At this point, Socrates distributes the roles and duties his interlocutors carry out. First, he excludes poets (*poiētikon genos*) from fulfilling this task since they are a *genos* of imitators (*mimētikon ethnos*). Above all, he aims to establish the *genos* authorized to say the truth against the *genos* of sophists:

> I am aware that the Sophists (*sophistōn genos*) have plenty of brave words and fair conceits, but I am afraid that being only wanderers from one city to another, and having never had habitations of their own (*oikēsis idias*), they may fail in their conception of philosophers and statesmen, and may not know what they do and say in time of war, when they are fighting or holding parley with their enemies. And thus people of your class (*genos*) are the only ones remaining who are fitted by nature and education to take part at once both in politics and philosophy.[18]

The true discourse about the polis can be performed only by the *genos* that has occupied permanently, since its birth, its original place. Derrida writes:

> Socrates privileges here again the *situation*, the relation to place: the genus of sophists is characterized by the absence of a proper place, an economy (*oikonomia*), a fixed domicile; these people have no domesticity. No house that is proper to them (*oikēsis idias*). They wander from place to place, from town to town, incapable of understanding these men who, being philosophers and politicians, *have (a)* place [*ont lieu*], that is, act by means of gesture and speech, in the city or at war.[19]

Therefore, the legitimacy of the discourses (*logoi*) authorized to state the truth of the *polis* depends on their belonging to a certain philosophical and political *genos*. The determination of this belonging, which provides the grounds for the very legitimacy of the true *logos*, is the determination of the belonging to one's own original place. This belonging refers to the order of dwelling, it is linked to the *oikos*, to the familiar nucleus as an original community, which is the constitutive element of the *polis*. Belonging is given by birth and education. It stands against one's differing from oneself that characterizes the *genos* of sophists, who wander from one city to another and have no proper place (*oikēsis idias*). At this point it is clear, or at least it should be, that the archaic ghost haunting ontology and politics and binding one to another comes from an archaic experience of dwelling and thus of community. This law imposes the task of thinking identity (ontological and political identity) in terms that are irreducibly spatial: origin as a place, permanence, stability, being distinguished and protected from difference, alterity, the stranger, and the foreign. Indeed, when opening his discourse on the origin and structure of the universe, Timaeus affirms the fundamental ontological distinction and defines the two opposite genera of being into which everything that is settles: the ideal and the sensible. Stability and permanence, immutable identity, are the ontological traits of the ideal being against the sensible being, which, conversely, corresponds to the order of becoming and thus is always changeable and differing from itself like the sophist.[20] At this point, it remains to show how this law also determines the ontological question of *khōra*.

The phantasm of the origin

Let me briefly summarize the context of the question: in the first part of his discourse, once the primary ontological distinction between the ideal and the sensible, between being and becoming has been posited, Timaeus introduces the figure of the Demiurge, who shapes the sensible by staring at the ideal. However, at the heart of his discourse, Timaeus wonders how this transition happens. He must hypothesize a third genus, neither ideal, nor sensible, through which the passage takes place, and he names it *khōra*. As it is neither sensible nor ideal, not even a being, it cannot be determined in any way as a being could be. For this reason, to describe it, Timaeus must use a set of analogies (the receptacle, the cast, the sieve, the nursemaid, etc.), assuming that none of them are adequate since they all come from the sensible determined in the *khōra*. This third remains indeterminate: the indeterminate that prevents itself from any possible determination and makes every determination possible. But, at the same time, in its indeterminateness *khōra* imposes on us the thought that all that is, is as such because it takes place, has an origin that remains fixed, permanent, and stable, has a proper place, *oikēsis idias*. In the aforementioned seminar, Derrida is more explicit:

> If *khōra* can receive everything, if it can become everything, one could ask why Timaeus insists on the necessity of a unique appellation. Perhaps, because it can receive everything, one could give it all the names one wants, since it can take any form, ultimately one could give a name different from *khōra*. As it does not exist under the form of a being identical with itself, of an ideal referent or a thing, one does not see why it would have only one name. But it is precisely because of this that it is always necessary to name it in the same way, since it is paradoxically necessary to keep the sense that it has no sense, to prevent one from puzzling it with what it receives and that it is not, so it is absolutely necessary for the law of discourse to name it always in the same constant and identifiable way in order not to confuse it with what it receives, with the forms it can take and, thus, it is necessary to name it always in the same way, it is necessary that language always points to that unique thing which is not a thing, which cannot be confused with anything, etc. Therefore, naming it in the same way means to maintain paradoxically the same reference

to what cannot ever be a real and determinate referent, a particular referent, a singular one.[21]

Referring to Critias's story about the act of the foundation of the city and, in particular, to Athena's choice of the place, the seminar explains that "this choice decides everything"[22] and thus highlights the first anticipation of the future, apparently ontological, question of *khōra*. Critias's discourse, Derrida remarks, "has already presented itself as a discourse about *khōra* even before *khōra* as such becomes the subject of the general discourse."[23] From this perspective, the choice of the name *khōra* seems to have been surreptitiously conditioned by the preamble to *Timaeus*, where Socrates summarizes the discourse about the ideal *polis*, and where the term first appears, long before Timaeus's onto-cosmogonic discourse. In the preamble, Socrates briefly describes the law that regulates weddings and education: it is necessary to raise the sons of the best citizens and take the others to another country, giving everybody their proper place. Socrates calls this place *khōran*.[24] In this first occurrence, *khōra*, according to its semantic specter, refers to the occupation of a place; it describes the borders of an inhabited territory *against* a wild space. Derrida writes:

> Although the word was already uttered (19a), the question of *khōra* as a general place or total receptacle is, of course, not *yet* posed. But if it is not posed as such, it gestures and points already. The note is given. For, on the one hand, the ordered polysemy of the word always includes the sense of political place or, more generally, of *invested* place, by opposition to abstract space. *Khōra* "means": place occupied by someone, country, inhabited Place, marked place, rank, post, assigned position, territory, or region. And in fact, Khōra *will* always already be occupied, invested, even as a general place, and even when it is distinguished from everything that takes place in it.[25]

Finally, for Plato, it is not important to establish what *khōra* is, but that there is a proper place, a unique origin that is self-identical, stable and permanent, an origin that, remaining indeterminate in itself, institutes the criterion of every possible ontological determination: identity understood as stability and permanence. Therefore, the law of the *oikos* secretly grounds ontology and thus our experience and conception of dwelling. It is a law but also an archaic phantasm to which no reality corresponds, since no reality can correspond to the myth of Erichthonius, the myth of autochthony, the myth of the political identity of Athens. This phantasm still haunts our experience and conception of dwelling and architecture.[26] Derrida refers to it in *Specters of Marx*, in a passage in which he proposes a formalization of its law:

> Inter-ethnic wars (have there ever been another kind?) are proliferating, driven by an archaic phantasm and concept, by a primitive conceptual phantasm of community, the nation-State, sovereignty, borders, native soil and blood. . . . But how can one deny that this conceptual phantasm is, so to speak, made more outdated than ever, in the very ontopology it supposes, by tele-technic dis-location? (By ontopology we mean an axiomatics linking indissociably the ontological value of present-being [on] to its *situation*, to the stable and presentable determination of a locality, the topos of territory, native soil, city, body in general).[27]

A little bit later, Derrida invites us to rethink dwelling in the wake of an experience of place and space that is more original than the experience imposed by the law of the *oikos*, an experience removed by the law of the *oikos* in the phantasmatic desire of an autochthonous identity, that is, of an identity pure and immune from any relation to the other in general: "All stability in a place being but a stabilization or a sedentarization, it will have to have been necessary that the local *différance*, the spacing of a displacement gives the movement its start. And gives place and gives rise [*donne place et donne lieu*]."[28]

This means that we must rethink dwelling by departing from *différance* as the condition of spacing and thus of taking place in general. This is the task of a deconstruction of the dwelling, and, at the same time, of the architecture of deconstruction.

2

THE HOUSE IN DECONSTRUCTION

Notes on Derrida and the Law of the Oikos

IN "THE LAW OF THE *OIKOS*," I ATTEMPTED TO DEMONSTRATE that a certain Greek experience of dwelling affects the institution of architecture as well as the construction of the metaphysics of presence in Plato. The stakes of *Khōra*, the text that Derrida proposes as a basis for his collaboration with Eisenman, is therefore the attachment of the identity of an individual and a community to a territory understood as the origin and foundation of this identity.[1] This conception is at work especially in the Athens of the archaic age and keeps on influencing classical Athens. The latter is the only Greek *polis* that is grounded on the myth of autochthony. In "The Law of the *Oikos*," I argued that, for Derrida, autochthony—a myth with a politico-religious function—organizes the very structure of Plato's *Timaeus*, once we recognize the role of this dialogue in the unaccomplished tryptic it was to belong to, alongside the *Critias* and the *Hermocrates*. In this order, the *Timaeus* must account for the onto-cosmological necessity that legitimates Athenian superiority over the other cities and thus the Platonic project of a refoundation on these bases. Here, I aim to engage in a deeper elaboration of the question of the "law of the *oikos*" as a mythico-religious matrix of the link between architecture and metaphysics by making even more explicit Derrida's reference to the Greek way of dwelling in "No (Point of) Madness—Maintaining Architecture."

The fortress in deconstruction

In "No (Point of) Madness—Maintaining Architecture," Derrida briefly indicates the features that link architecture to a series or constellations of mutually solidary values. They are drawn from a historical origin and yet so rooted as to remain immutable for the time to come:

> The concept of architecture is itself an inhabited *constructum*, a legacy that understands us even before we try to think it. Certain invariants remain through all the mutations of architecture. Impassable, imperturbable, an axiomatic traverses the whole history of architecture. An axiomatic, that is to say, an organized whole of fundamental and always presupposed evaluations. This hierarchy has fixed itself in stone; henceforth, it informs the entirety of social space. What are these invariants? I will distinguish four, the slightly artificial charter of four traits, let us say, rather, of four points.[2]

All four articulations through which we can grasp the invariance of this axiomatic throughout its very historical explanation refer to the Greek soil.[3] Indeed, the first one, the law of the *oikos*, seems to have a particular privilege with respect to the other three: it seems to be the matrix that contains the others as germs:

> The experience of meaning must be the *dwelling* [habitation], the law of the *oikos*, the economy of men or gods. . . . the architectural work seems to have been destined for the presence of men and gods. The arrangement, occupation, and investment of locations should be measured against this economy. Heidegger once again recalls this economy when he interprets homelessness (*Heimatlosigkeit*) as the symptom of

ontotheology and, more precisely, of modern technology. . . . This is not a deconstruction, but rather a call to repeat the very grounds of the architecture that we inhabit, that we should relearn how to inhabit, the origin of its meaning. . . . Centered and hierarchized, the architectural organization will have had to fall in line with the anamnesis of its origin and the basis of a foundation. Not only from the time of its founding on the ground of the earth, but also since its juridico-political founding, the institution that commemorates the myths of the city, the heroes or founding gods. Despite appearances, this religious or political memory, this historicism, has not deserted modern architecture. Modern architecture is still nostalgic for it: it is its destiny to be a guardian. An always hierarchizing nostalgia: architecture will have materialized this hierarchy in stone or wood (*hylē*); *it* is a hyletics of the sacred (*hieros*) and the principle (*archē*), an *archihieratics*.

—This economy remains, of necessity, a *teleology* of dwelling. It subscribes to all the regimes of finality. Ethico-political purposiveness, religious duty, utilitarian or functional ends: it is always a matter of putting architecture *in service*, and *at the service of*. This end is the principle of the archihieratic order.

—Whatever its mode, period, or dominant style, this order ultimately depends on the *fine arts*. The value of beauty, harmony, and totality must still reign.[4]

A few pages by Jean-Pierre Vernant allow us to reconstruct the elliptical traces left by Derrida in this passage. In particular, Vernant highlights in a precise fashion the role that architecture plays in the transition of Greek civilization from the Mycenaean age to the archaic one, through which it had been constituting a political space that was essentially new with respect to the one governed by the Mycenaean king, the incarnation of the politico-religious identity of sovereignty sheltered in the *megaron* building that centralizes and regulates all the activities of the community. The new politico-religious space that comes out of the ruins of the earlier space will find its fulfillment in the classical age as the space of the *polis*, the city-state:

> The religious system is profoundly reorganized in connection with the new forms of social life represented by the city, the *polis*. . . . Without taking stock of all the religious innovations produced by the archaic age, we must at least signal the most important ones. Above all, the appearance of the temple as a construction independent of the human habitat, real palace, or particular house. Thanks to a belt delimiting the sacred area (*temenos*) and an external altar, the temple constitutes a building separated from the profane space. The god permanently lies there through the intermediary of a great cultural and anthropomorphic statue that is fixed there permanently (*fixée à demeure*). Other than domestic altars and private sanctuaries, this "house of god" is public, a good shared by all citizens. Consecrated to the divinity, it can no longer belong but to the city itself, which erected it in precise places, in order to mark and confirm its legitimate domination over a territory: at the center of the city, Acropolis, or agora; at the doors that surround the urban agglomerate and in their proximity; in the area of the *agros* and of the *eschatiai*, of wild territories and borders, which separates each Greek city from the neighbors. Organizing the space of sacred places, establishing the path of ritual processions, from the center to the periphery, mobilizing at fixed dates, back and forth, the entire population or part of it, the building of a network of urban, sub-, and extra-urban sanctuaries, aims to shape the surface of the soil according to a religious order. Through the

mediation of its civic god installed in the temples, the community establishes a sort of symbiosis between the man and the territory as if citizens were the sons of an earth from which they were born at the origins under the condition of autochthony and which, thanks to this intimate link with those who inhabit it, is lifted to the level of a legitimate "civic earth." Therefore, we can explain the harshness of the conflicts that between the VIII and VI centuries opposed neighbors for the appropriation of the places of cult at the frontiers, which sometimes were shared by two cities. The occupation of the sanctuary and its cultural link to the urban center count as a legitimate possession. When the polis founds its temples, it pushes its roots up to the divine world in order to grant a firm foundation to its territorial base.[5]

From the perspective of the history of architecture, Rykwert also highlights the radical novelty of the Greek temple by recurring to expressions similar to Vernant's. For Rykwert, however, the most important novelty consists in the elaboration of a constructive typology that is determinate in its minimal details—the introduction of the orders—and thus in the constitution of a technico-artistic discipline endowed with norms and protocols that have to be applied by a category of specialized craftsmen, somehow independently from local conditions:

> The architectural improvement of the largest, or at least richest, settlements, which is based on the repetition of certain forms and planning procedures, seems to confirm the existence of an organization of paid specialized constructors (*demiurgoi*). The wide diffusion of architectural typologies and structural techniques in the first century of the Olympic age could also testify that these constructors move, like metalworkers, from one city to another.[6]

The Greek temple thus attests to the birth of architecture as the codified technico-artistic discipline of the specialized architect, whose social position is recognized as privileged because of the material and symbolic value of the work this specialist does for the *polis*. We can begin to understand the perspective Derrida adopts, the reason why he proposes the reading of the *Timaeus* to Eisenman, a dialogue in which the figure of the *demiurge* as the architect of the universe appears. The cult of heroes evoked by Derrida emerges precisely in this context and demarcates the role played by architecture in the *polis*. Here Vernant finds an analogous politico-religious function that is emphasized even more, establishing the bind that ties the identity of the community to a determinate place, through a foundational myth of recent invention. In this case, too, the role played by architecture is essential, as a place of recollection of the mythical and not historical foundation of the city linked to the territory:

> Another change, whose meaning is partially analogous, will deeply mark the religious system. It is in the VIII century that the habit of reactivating the Mycenaean constructions develops rapidly, especially the funerary constructions, left unused for centuries. Once restructured, they serve as places of cult for funerary honors made to legendary figures, almost always without relationship with these buildings and yet claiming for their noble lineage, *genè*. [. . .] Even more than the cult of gods, even of civic gods, the cult of heroes has a civic as well as territorial value: it is associated with a precise place, a tomb with the underground presence of the defunct, whose remains were often found far away and brought back to their place. Tombs and heroic cults, through the prestige of the honored hero, play for the community the role of glorious symbols and talismans, whose place is often kept secret as the safety of the State depends

on its protection. Settled in the heart of the city, in the agora, they embody the memory of the more or less legendary founder of the city, the *archegetes* hero and, in the case of a colony, the founding hero. [. . .] Their function is that of gathering together (*rassembler*) a group around the cult whose exclusiveness belongs to the group itself and that appears installed in a precise place of the soil.[7]

In the classical age, the organization of public space, where political life takes place, the agora, demarcates itself from the properly religious space, and yet the latter keeps on playing the fundamental role given to it in the archaic age, that of tying the identity of the community to the delimitation of the territory through the cult of protective divinities and hero-founders. Temples and sanctuaries are still the places of worship in the city, where the memory of a mythical foundation is guarded for the time to come, thus legitimating the possession of a determinate territory.[8] It is by these fundamental values that Pericles's project is inspired for the realization of a great monumental sanctuary in Athens, bound to affirm the identity and greatness of the *polis*, the legitimacy of its claims for hegemony in front of the other peoples, Greek and foreigners. The Acropolis of Athens is the place where the palace of the Mycenaean age surged, that is, the politico-religious fortress governing the surrounding territory from on high. It is the place where in the archaic age the first urban settlement was constituted, a settlement whose expansion precipitated the construction of new walls for its defense and protection. As Athenian politics transformed, from Solon on, the role of the Acropolis too changed, from city to sanctuary, to the symbolic place of the identity of the city. Built on the originary site, it guards the memory of its foundation rooted in myth, through the cult of Athena, the protective divinity, and Erichthonius, the hero-founder born from the earth, which constitutes the myth of the autochthony of the Athenian ethnicity. It is because of this symbolic value that the Athenian Acropolis will be conquered and destroyed by the Persians (480 BC)[9] and reconstructed as soon as the political conditions made it possible.[10] To affirm the recovered greatness of the city, but also to remove the recent trauma of being destroyed by a foreign people, first Cimon and then Pericles will allocate enormous investments to restore to the Acropolis its value as the symbolic place of the identity of the community and the legitimacy of its hegemony over the Greek people.[11]

To carry out his symbolico-political project, Pericles calls Phidias, the greatest plastic artist of the time. He will supervise the general project of the site and realize with his disciples the metopes of the Parthenon, the temple designed first by Callicrates and then by Ictinus, devoted to Athena, the virgin goddess protector of the city, long considered the highest example of the Doric order. If many other architects were involved in the realization of single buildings that compose the sanctuary, Phidias designs the urban setting that organizes the symbolic path and the stages of the great procession that leads the entire population along the sacred way, during the Pan-Athenians, the feast of the city, from the urban settlement up to the ascension of the sanctuary, the Parthenon and thus to the great altar of Athena. Here the city offers sacrifices to the goddess and its peplos, the dress woven again each time, with the embroidered scenes of the myth that links the goddess to the protection of the city. The procession is also represented, idealized through figures of a divine procession, on the Ionic frieze running along the walls of the temple, a relief also attributed to the genius of Phidias. Therefore, it is on the Acropolis that the artistic skills, the mastery of aesthetic-formal orders as well as of the effects of the collective imagery—beauty, harmony, and totality—merge in a broad architectural project, serving a precise political project: legitimating the "juridico-political ground" of the city-state, tying the latter to a territorial ground through the symbolic elaboration of a religious and mythical foundation, of an "archihieratics." This project is bound to become the paradigm of architecture and more generally of Western culture. It is therefore in Athens, on the Acropolis, that we should look for the determination of architecture as the last fortress of metaphysics. It is in this determination of architecture that metaphysics finds its ultimate and perhaps impregnable dwelling. The place itself says so: *acropolis* means the high town and refers to the fortified city, heir of the royal fortress of the Mycenaean age.[12] If Athens is the only Greek city where the continuity of the Mycenaean civilization is not brutally interrupted it is thanks to the role that the Acropolis had always played in it, despite political transformations.[13]

Indeed, the Athens of Pericles is also that of Plato. Here, the philosopher was born a few years after the death of Pericles, and this is the city, already in crisis, tormented by interminable internal conflicts, a city that the adult Plato aims to found again from the origins. This is the city Socrates never leaves, not even to escape the death penalty inflicted by the city itself. The city inhabited by Plato as well as inhabiting Plato, as Derrida invites us to think in "No (Point of) Madness—Maintaining Architecture," when he refers to the symbolic and material force the city exercises on its citizens, through its architecture, thus affecting their experience and existence. It is in this space that the Platonic corpus is inscribed and articulated. It is here that the whole of the mythico-religious value of Greek civilization is reinscribed, reelaborated, amended, and reorganized within the conceptual system of metaphysics, in view of creating the "law of the *oikos*" that still governs our architectural culture.

3

JACQUES DERRIDA AND THE POLITICS OF ARCHITECTURE

"THE LAST FORTRESS OF METAPHYSICS": THIS IS HOW DERRIDA designates architecture in "No (Point of) Madness—Maintaining Architecture."[1] This work is published in 1986 and accompanies the presentation of the project devised by Bernard Tschumi for the La Villette park in Paris. It is the first text Derrida dedicates to architecture.

My aim is to show how the deconstruction of architecture set in motion by Derrida not only concerns the theory of architecture. It also displays the possibility of a different architectural practice, which cannot be identified with a new aesthetic and formal style. Indeed, the deconstruction of architecture entails the deconstruction of the political and can be carried out only through the actual deconstruction of the architectural structure in which the Western tradition of the political has embodied itself. This tradition is grounded on the relation that links the identity of the individual and the community to a supposedly originary space, to the stability of the frontiers that separate it from otherness in general, from what is therefore conceived of, simultaneously or alternately, as external, foreign, stranger, and strange.

In *Specters of Marx* (1993) Derrida names ontopology the fundamental structure of the political, as it ties together the ontological and metaphysical value of presence—*on*—and the place—*topos*—: "By ontopology we mean an axiomatic linking indissociably the ontological value of present-being (on) to its *situation*, to the stable and presentable determination of a locality, the *topos* of territory, native soil, city, body in general."[2] The essence of the political therefore has been linked since the beginning to the politics of space and place. In "Plato's Pharmacy," holding on to the deconstruction of Platonic philosophy, Derrida remarks that, since Plato, the system of oppositions governing our philosophical tradition has hinged on the undisputed presupposition of a spatial opposition:

> In order for these contrary values (good/evil, true/false, essence/appearance, inside/outside, etc.) to be in opposition, each of the terms must be simply *external* to the other, which means that one of these oppositions (the opposition between inside and outside) must already be accredited as the matrix of all possible opposition. And one of the elements of the system (or of the series) must also stand as the very possibility of systematicity or seriality in general.[3]

In particular, with regard to the *polis*, the practice of ostracism and the related rituals of the purification of the city, Derrida highlights the intimate correlation among political identity, urban topology, and the exclusion of the other, which rests on the spatial opposition inside/outside:

> The city's body *proper* thus reconstitutes its unity, closes around the security of its inner courts, gives back to itself the word that links it with itself within the confines of the agora, by violently excluding from its territory the representative of an external threat or aggression. That representative represents the otherness of the evil that comes to affect or infect the inside by unpredictably breaking into it. Yet the representative of the outside is nonetheless *constituted*, regularly granted its place by the community, chosen, kept, fed, etc., in the very heart of the inside.[4]

In the Western tradition, the (individual and collective) identity is thought as an internal, permanent, stable space, autonomous and independent from the other in general, which is represented as external and foreign and thus is experienced as a possible threat. Going back to *Specters of Marx*, Derrida argues that this axiomatic continues to structure political discourse and action today: it is always at work where we appeal to the defense of territorial identity against the other, which is lived or rather represented as the external threat that justifies the closure from inside. As this axiomatic goes back to the origin of Greek civilization and thus of the Western tradition, Derrida recognizes the return of a "conceptual specter," an "archaism."[5] This axiomatic appears today as a reaction, since it is constituted as a fortress against the process of deterritorialization that is not only related to the migratory flows pressing Western frontiers but also to the conditions of development of economic and cultural relations and exchanges, to the constitution of a public space that is in principle unlimited and, therefore, to the life itself we want to protect.[6] Nowadays, finally, the relation to the other, lived as a threat to the community, turns out to be, at the same time, the irreducible condition of the life of the community. The place turns out to be what it has always been: not the mythical origin of metaphysical identity, but the effect of a process of dislocation and localization where the anthropic presence inscribes itself into space, situates itself, in any case, in relation to otherness in general and thus by dividing itself from the outset:

> The process of dislocation is no less arch-originary, that is, just as "archaic" as the archaism that it has always dislodged. This process is, moreover, the positive condition of the stabilization that it constantly relaunches. All stability in a place being but a stabilization or a sedentarization, it will have to have been necessary that a local *différance*, the spacing of a displacement gives the movement its start. And gives place and gives rise (*donne place et donne lieu*).[7]

Therefore, we should think space not as the surface where originary places, being self-enclosed and forever established, are distributed, but as the element of the relation to otherness, where there is a possible individual and collective localization that, for this reason, cannot be closed to the other in general, to the relation that constitutes every identity as the effect of an irreducible opening. To have space for the other, to give place to this relation, is the task of the deconstruction of the political. This does not simply mean to value the other as such, always and anyhow. The horizon of the relation to the other always entails a threat to the life of the community, independently of the forms this threat takes on. History, even in recent years, does not stop making us face this cruel reality: terroristic, colonial, or postcolonial conflicts among states or within a state. However, as the relation to the other is the irreducible condition of possibility of the community, to avoid, subdue, repress, or remove such a relation would mean to expose the community to an even more severe threat. At least, this is so for a community that aims to be democratic, for which the responsibility of this opening, the always open possibility of its own transformation, is life itself.[8]

Housing politics

To have space for the other, to give a place to this relation, is the task of the deconstruction of the political. The accomplishment of this task necessarily requires the deconstruction of the architecture that provides the axiomatics at issue with a concrete and durable form, with a form that imposes itself onto our experience as if it were our natural environment. We may think of the structure of the city, of the hierarchic layout of the institutional, economic, religious, symbolic, residential sites that constitute the identity of the community, and, at the same time, mark times and manners of our individual and collective daily experience. At this point, we can go back to the aforementioned essay on architecture. According to Derrida, architecture is the last fortress of metaphysics precisely because it sets up a concrete, established, and durable shape for identity, which is conceived of as a familiar and self-enclosed interiority or intimacy, engaged with the defense of itself. This identity has been determined since the origin by the analogy with a specific kind of architectural structure: the house/dwelling. In fact, if nowadays we consider natural the fact that dwelling is the end and essence of architecture, this is because, since the origin of metaphysics, namely, from Plato on, architecture has been submitted to the law of dwelling, of the *oikos*: dwelling as a protection of the inside from the outside, of the familiar from the stranger. The house is built in defense of the institution of the patriarchal family, according to a precise spatial distribution of roles in relation to the management of the property. The man, the head of the family, open to the outside, is in charge of accumulating and exchanging goods, while the woman, closed inside, deals with the administration of stockpiled goods. The former is active in public life; the latter is connected with the worship of forefathers:[9]

> Let us never forget that there is an architecture of architecture. Down even to its archaic foundation, the most fundamental concept of architecture has been *constructed*. This naturalized architecture is bequeathed to us: we inhabit it, it inhabits us, we think it is destined for habitation, and it is no longer an object for us at all. But we must recognize in it an *artifact*, a *construction*, a monument. . . . Its heritage inaugurates the intimacy of our economy, the law of our hearth (*oikos*), our familial, religious, and political oikonomy, all the places of birth and death, temple, school, stadium, agora, square, sepulcher. It goes right through us to the point that we forget its very historicity: we take it for nature.[10]

Therefore, from the outset, the metaphysics of presence has used a certain model of architectural building—the house—to determine the meaning of individual and collective identity. For this reason, dwelling represents the end and essence our tradition has assigned to architecture. Today we still acknowledge this as obvious and undisputable. Architecture still represents the concrete accomplishment of the aforementioned model, the most resistant and effective one to the extent that it does not only affect our way of thinking but also our most immediate experience.

> On the other hand, architecture forms its most powerful metonymy; it gives it its most solid *consistency*, objective substance. By consistency, I do not mean only logical coherence, which implicates all dimensions of human experience in the same network: there is no work of architecture without interpretation, or even economic, religious political, aesthetic, or philosophical decision. But by consistency I also mean duration, hardness, the monumental, mineral, or ligneous subsistence, the hyletics of tradition. Hence the *resistance*. The resistance of materials like the resistance of consciousness and unconsciousness that establishes this architecture as the last fortress of metaphysics.[11]

However, the law of dwelling, as old as it is, is not an immutable law of nature. It corresponds to a historically determinate order, the order of the metaphysics of presence that still governs our notion of individual and collective identity through the strong and durable form granted by architecture. Therefore, the law of dwelling can be transformed, deconstructed, in view of another experience of individual and collective identity. So it is necessary to emancipate the theory and praxis of architecture, the experience itself of architecture from the link that subordinates it to the law of the house and dwelling:

> A consistent deconstruction would be nothing if it did not take account of this resistance and this transference; it would do little if it did not take on architecture as much as the architectonic. To take it on: not in order to attack, destroy, or lead it astray, to criticize or disqualify it. Rather, in order to *think* it in fact, to take sufficient distance from it so as to apprehend it in a thought that carries beyond the theorem—and becomes an oeuvre in turn.[12]

The deconstruction of architecture must in turn become work, it must become architecture.

Architecture to come

But how should we build the architecture of deconstruction? In the essay we are reading here, Derrida does not provide us with clear instructions. He raises a question and leaves it open as only architecture can respond: "Is an architecture of events possible?"[13] My aim is to demonstrate that here Derrida does not call for an architecture that would produce a media or artistic event. I will explain that, through the question of the event, Derrida means to trace architecture back to its irreducible responsibilities. He draws attention to the ethico-political implications of architectural practice. To understand this perspective, we must take into account other texts by Derrida devoted to architecture, which are perhaps less known but equally meaningful. In a long interview with David Wills and Peter Brunette, Derrida answers a question concerning the call for an affirmative architecture, launched at the end of "Fifty-Two Aphorisms for a Foreword": "The without-ground of a deconstructive and affirmative architecture can cause vertigo, but it is not the void, it is not the gaping and chaotic remainder, the hiatus of destruction."[14] In the interview, Derrida explains what he meant with this apparently enigmatic call:

BRUNETTE You point to this affirmative place in your work, but you never name it. Can this place be named?

DERRIDA It's not a place; it's not a place that really exists. It's a 'come' [*viens*]; it is what I call an affirmation that is not positive. It doesn't exist, it isn't present. I always distinguish affirmation from the position of a positivity. Thus it is an affirmation that is very risky, uncertain, improbable; it entirely escapes the space of certainty.[15]

Yet, before explaining how we should understand this call for an event to come beyond the horizon of certainty, Derrida points out that the call for the event of an affirmative architecture must be inscribed in an ethico-political dimension. It concerns the possibilities of our being together:

Before coming back to that, since you quoted that passage, I can say that I insist on this point in the text on architecture for two reasons: first, because in fact people can say that deconstructive architecture is absurd because architecture constructs. So it is necessary to explain what the term means in the text, that 'deconstructive architecture' refers precisely to what happens in terms of 'gathering', the being together, the assembly, the now [*maintenant*], the maintaining. Deconstruction does not consist simply of dissociating or disarticulating or destroying, but of affirming a certain 'being together', a certain *maintenant*; construction is possible only to the extent that the foundations themselves have been deconstructed. Affirmation, decision, invention, the coming about the *constructum* is not possible unless the philosophy of architecture, the history of architecture, the foundations themselves have been questioned.

If the foundations are assured, there is no construction; neither is there any invention. Invention assumes an undecidability; it assumes that at a given moment there is nothing. We found on the basis of non-foundation. Thus deconstruction is the condition of construction, of true invention, of a real affirmation that holds something together, that constructs. From this point of view, only deconstruction, only a certain appeal to or call by deconstruction, can really invent architecture.[16]

Therefore, the architecture of the event must be the affirmation of an architecture able to give place to the invention of an absolutely new being together. This call for an absolute novelty may seem a politico-revolutionary statement, but its necessity is rooted in the structural conditions of any responsible decision, namely, in the ethical dimension of our being together:

Now what is this call? I don't know. If I knew, nothing would ever happen. The fact is, in order for what we conveniently call deconstruction to get off the ground, that call is necessary. It says 'come' [*viens*], but come where, I don't know. Where this call comes from, and from whom, I don't know. That doesn't simply mean that I am an ignorant; it is heterogeneous to knowledge. In order for that call to exist, the order of knowledge must be breached. If we can identify, objectify, recognize the place, from that moment on there is no call. In order for there to be a call, . . . the orders of determination and of knowledge must be exceeded. It is in relation to non-knowledge that the call is made. Thus I do not have a response. I can't tell you 'this is it'. I truly don't know, but this 'I don't know' doesn't just result from ignorance, or skepticism, or nihilism, or obscurantism. This non-knowledge is the necessary condition for something to happen, for responsibility to be taken, for a decision to be made, for an event to take place.[17]

Certainly, a naive reader would take this explanation as more enigmatic than the formulation it is supposed to account for. A certain acquaintance with Derrida's treatment of the notion of the event is required. This notion implies by itself an ethical dimension, as we can see from the fact that here Derrida ties the possibility of responsibility and decision to the possibility of the event. Indeed, responsibility and decision are exemplary manifestations of ethical acts. In *The Politics of Friendship*, we can find a clear definition:

> The instant of decision must remain heterogeneous to all knowledge as such, to all theoretical or reportive determination, even if it may and must be preceded by all possible science and conscience. The latter are unable to determine the leap of decision without transforming it into the irresponsible application of a program, hence without depriving it of what makes it a sovereign and free decision—in a word, of what makes it a decision, if there is one.[18]

Here Derrida says that a responsible decision, in order to be such, must respond to the order of the event and thus must be something absolutely new and unpredictable with respect to what is known and shared. It must not be the consequence of a calculation, the mere application of a known and shared rule, but must imply the individual and personal exposure of the one who takes on the responsibility. The responsible decision must be absolutely mine in order to be responsible. For this reason, a certain nonknowledge is necessarily implied in the responsible decision. More radically, every responsible decision must be grounded on this nonknowledge because it has always been taken toward others:

How is the *question of the response* to be linked to the question of responsibility? . . . One says 'to answer to', 'to respond to', 'to answer before'. These three modalities are not juxtaposable; they are enveloped and implied in one another. One *answers for*, for self or for something (for someone, for an action, a thought, a discourse), *before*—before an other, a community of others, an institution, a court, a law. And always one *answers for* (for self or for its intention, its action or discourse), *before*, by first responding *to*: this last modality thus appearing more originary, more fundamental and hence unconditional.[19]

According to Derrida, this relationship with the other is the proper dimension of ethics: the respect for the other is such only if the relationship with the other is able to account for the irreducible alterity of the other. The encounter with the other must be irreducible to my categories. If I project onto the other what I already know, if I reduce it to the case of a well-known generality, I deny the other its irreducible alterity. To this extent, the encounter with the other must respond to the order of the event. At this point, you may wonder how architecture is related to these issues. In fact, the relation to the other depends on the fact that there are spaces and places where the other could be encountered and welcomed in its irreducible alterity. In the literature dedicated to Derrida's work on this point, in particular, to the seminars about hospitality, the foreigner is commonly seen as the exemplary figure of this irreducible alterity appealing to our responsibility.[20] However, there is a more radical and irreducible alterity, which, at the same time, concerns us more closely, toward which architecture has an enormous responsibility: the other to come, that is, the alterity of the so-called future generations. Toward this figure of alterity it is easier to admit the condition of irreducible non-knowledge in which we find ourselves as well as architecture, when it makes buildings bound to resist time. We don't know who comes after us, we don't know when, but we know that someone will come, or, rather, we are responsible for the coming of those who will come after us, we are responsible for the conditions by which the other to come can come, and finally for the fact that there are conditions by which there is a to-come for the other, and thus the other has place. This question is nowadays more evident than ever. According to Derrida, it concerns architecture but is not acknowledged as such in architectural practice. He discusses this point in two, perhaps not well known, texts that share an analogous and chronologically close topic: a) the paper given at the Berlinstadtforum, a public forum devoted to the discussion of the reconstruction of Berlin after the fall of the wall;[21] b) the paper presented at a conference in Prague organized around the same subject, the future of the city.[22] The two papers were written in 1991. I will refer to the latter text, since the former is the record of a public discussion in which also other interlocutors take part (for instance, Wim Wenders). I suggest that *Wings of Desire* (*Der Himmel über Berlin*) was somehow influenced by this conversation with Derrida.

The Prague paper is certainly more articulate and interesting. It begins by relating the question addressed to all the speakers: "Which future for Prague?" namely, the question of responsibility:

> Before whom, before which memory and which to-come, before and for which generation are we responsible when we take the responsibility of a city? My hypothesis is that the answer to this question binds us to modify slightly the concept of responsibility. Any project regarding the destiny of a city, that is, what ties its memory with its present and to-come exceeds for essential reasons the possibility of accomplishment as well as the dimension of a generation, a nationality, or a language. Time calls for a promise engaging even more than one generation and, thus, more than

a politics, more than politics, in a duration the heterogeneity, discontinuity, and non-totalization of which must be accepted as a law.[23]

To explain the sense of this hypothesis, Derrida proposes a reading of Kafka's story "The City Coat of Arms." Here Kafka tells of an imaginary city, which can easily be identified with Prague, whose destiny is linked to the project of building a tower able to touch the sky, something like the tower of Babel. This figure embodies the original architectural impulse, the political imperative to which architecture has always been called to respond: the construction of symbols of the collective identity bound to endure over time:

> People argued in this way: The essential thing in the whole business is the idea of building a tower that will reach to heaven. In comparison with that idea everything else is secondary. The idea, once seized in its magnitude, can never vanish again; so long as there are men on the earth, there will be also the irresistible desire to complete the building.[24]

Since the project required a collective effort that exceeded the possibility of completing it in a short time, it was necessary to found a city for the workmen. However, the construction of the city, which reproduced the divisions among the various nationalities that were working at the tower, provoked a series of conflicts:

> That being so, however, one need have no anxiety about the future; on the contrary, human knowledge is increasing, the art of building has made progress and will make further progress, a piece of work which takes us a year may perhaps be done in half the time in another hundred years, and better done, too, more enduringly. So why exert oneself to the extreme limit of one's present powers? There

would be some sense in doing that only if it were likely that the tower could be completed in one generation. But that is beyond all hope. It is far more likely that the next generation with their perfected knowledge will find the work of their predecessors bad, and tear down what has been built so as to begin anew. Such thoughts paralyzed people's powers, and so they were troubled less about the tower than the construction of a city for the workmen. Every nationality wanted the finest quarters for itself, and this gave rise to disputes, which developed into bloody conflicts. These conflicts never came to an end; to the leaders they were a new proof that, in the absence of the necessary unity, the building of the tower must be done very slowly, or indeed preferably postponed until universal peace was declared. But the time was spent not only in conflict; the town was embellished in the intervals, and this unfortunately enough evoked fresh envy and fresh conflict. In this fashion the age of the first generation went past, but none of the succeeding ones showed any difference; except that technical skill increased and with it occasion for conflict. To this must be added that the second or third generation had already recognized the senselessness of building a heaven-reaching tower; but by that time everybody was too deeply involved to leave the city.[25]

According to Derrida, we can draw from this story a lesson for architecture:

> This surplus, this plurality of idioms, interpreters, nations, these ceaseless wars let one think that the essence of a city is somewhere else or more precisely it is other than the tower. It is by renouncing to the tower, the highest ambition of a unique tower, of a capital erection touching the sky that, in few generations,

a community shapes itself in the renunciation itself and takes the decision to maintain the city precisely in place of an impossible tower. And this responsible decision is taken in the name of the to-come. One renounces to the totalitarian project of tower, dismantles the idea of tower precisely when one becomes aware of the fact that what counts is the opening to the promise and, thus, to the to-come. What is catastrophic in the design of a city is the wish to solve all problems exhaustively by the term of a generation, without given time and space to the generations to come, leaving them time and space as a legacy, precisely because those who-know-how, architects and urban planner, believe to know in advance what tomorrow will be and therefore replace the ethico-political responsibility with their techno-scientific programming.[26]

At this point we can understand what the responsibility of architecture consists in, a responsibility that the architecture to-come must take up: that of the very possibility of the to-come, of the to-come of an alterity that must remain irreducible, and thus of generations to come to whom the present should grant the chance or, rather, space and places to show up, dwell, live according their own conditions. The legacy of architecture and urban planning we are used to is heavy: designing, planning, and building up for the time to come. Architecture fills the space for whoever comes and who we don't know. For this reason, Derrida believes that architecture must reckon with an irreducible nonknowledge concerning alterity and the to-come of anyone who comes, without, therefore, refusing to build, without refusing the task of building for the to-come, to keep open the space to come, the space of the relation to the other, which is vital for us:

A city is a whole which must keep indefinitely and structurally non-saturable, open to its own transformation, to additions that come to alter or dislocate as much as possible the memory of the heritage. A city must keep open to the fact that it knows that it does not know how it will be: it is necessary to inscribe the respect of this knowledge in science and in the architectural and urbanistic expertise. Otherwise, what would one do but applying programs, totalizing, saturating, suturing, asphyxiating? And without taking any responsible decision. For accomplishing a program or putting a design to work is never a responsible decision.[27]

By not building, architecture would fail short of the responsibility to prepare the space for the coming of the to-come. We should think and practice an architecture able to expose itself to its transformation to come. To render this perspective plausible, at least for the West, Derrida conjures up the example of the temple of Ise in Japan, the most remarkable place of worship of Shintoism. The temple has been dismantled and rebuilt with new materials every twenty years for one thousand five hundred years. The next time will be in 2033. The community renews and refounds itself through this ritual construction. Is the place, in Western culture, for an architecture that implies in its project and construction the possibility of being renewed or radically modified, confirmed or rebuilt by other builders, the builders to come? It is only according to this perspective that architecture can keep open the chance of the relation to the other, a chance that is the necessary condition for the other to live and take place, to be what it is, unless the community is captive within the walls it has erected to reject the other and to defend a pure but empty interiority, which has no future. I conclude with a quotation from Derrida's last contribution to the symposiums organized by "Anyone Corporation," in Japan in 1992. His paper, entitled "Faxtexture," ends by announcing the necessity to think another space, a space opened toward others and the event of the other to come, and thus toward the necessity to deconstruct, through architecture, the ontopological axiomatics in view of the very future of the political, in the name of a democracy to come:

> How is it possible to re-politicize the architectural theory or practice just de-constructing a certain concept of the political, even of democracy? The question may disclose enormous and unending tasks, but it must remain open: that is a necessity and an obligation. This "must" is more original and important than the question it bears and makes possible. *It gives the question its opening.* It cannot be but the opening to the other, to the other to which it addresses itself or *from where it comes*; opening from the other and to the other and, thus, to the future, to the otherness that cannot be anticipated, to the possibility of surprise without which there would be no opening. Deconstruction, or if you like, re-building, does not only get through discourses. It proceeds also from what is coming and has not come yet, through events and inventions. Future, invention, event, that require a re-politicizing deconstruction of the political, must *open* calculus, project, program, rule and law on what must remain non-calculable. To open them does not mean to put them out of play or destroy them. It has to do with another gesture, another movement, another relation to space.[28]

4

MYTHOGRAPHIES

Toward an Architectural Writing

LITERALLY SPEAKING, THE ENGAGEMENT WITH ARCHITECture seems to circumscribe a limited moment of Derrida's work, caused by a series of occasional episodes. I aim to demonstrate that, beyond the letter, the writing of deconstruction seems to elaborate a decisive configuration with architecture. We should take into serious consideration "No (Point of) Madness—Maintaining Architecture," the text that systematically traces the path followed by Derrida throughout his writings and interventions on architecture. In this text, he defines architecture as the "last fortress of metaphysics"[1] and calls for the urgency of a deconstruction of architecture. The effectiveness of architecture itself would depend on the possibility of its deconstruction. This possibility is not merely theoretical but above all practical: the deconstruction of architecture must become a work, must happen through architecture and, in turn, be architecture. How would this architecture be? This question seems to press the architect, more than one architect. It should also press Derrida's readers since, as I aim to show, it is intimately linked to Derrida's writing, to the necessity of the writing adopted by Derrida as well as of taking account beyond some stereotypes that have only served to evade the problem.[2]

From architecture to writing

In "No (Point of) Madness—Maintaining Architecture," Derrida finds the possibility of the architecture of deconstruction in the work of Bernard Tschumi. This possibility is what Derrida calls *the writing of space*. I quote: "the imminence of what is happening to us now [*de ce qui nous arrive maintenant*] announces not only an architectural event [*événement*]: rather a writing of space, a mode of spacing that makes a place for the event [*un mode d'espacement qui fait sa place à l'événement*]."[3] This passage is difficult. Each word should be taken into careful consideration: from "writing of space" to its first declension ("a mode of spacing").

Along this path, I aim to show that we do not understand what the architecture of deconstruction is if we do not come back to the decisive notion of *arche-writing*. Derrida recurs to the latter to account for the irreducible condition of possibility of experience and thus for the condition of possibility of the elaboration of meaning, independently of the form of this elaboration: verbal language, ideogram, pictogram, hieroglyphic, phonetico-alphabetic writing, or abstract notation such as mathematical or architectural signs. As is well known, Derrida had developed this notion from his earliest texts, in particular, in *Of Grammatology*. In these texts, Derrida affirms the necessity of remodulating arche-writing through practices of meaning that would be different from the ones regulated by the hegemonic processes of signification in our tradition. The latter hinges on the determination of writing as a mere instrument in the service of the empirical transmission of significations that are supposedly constituted by themselves within the intimacy of an ipseity (according to a historical stratification: *psyche*, soul, subject, speculative or intentional consciousness, etc.).

Following this order, writing would be the mere, empirical instrument designated for the spatial and thus external representation of the temporal flux of speech, the privileged element of the expression of meaning, the very element of the *logos*, of the major tradition of philosophy, namely, Western thought, as Derrida had demonstrated since his earliest work. Finally, according to this traditional conception, writing participates in the processes of signification only to the extent that it is subordinated to the ideal of linear phonetico-alphabetic writing. In the pages from *Of Grammatology* to which I will refer, Derrida explains that this ideal is neither necessary nor universal; it has historically imposed itself through the removal of other possible modulations of arche-writing, of other historically given practices of the inscription of meaning. This ideal is now in deconstruction. However, this deconstruction does not so much consist in going back to primordial practices of writing as in showing that the possibilities of a different modulation of arche-writing are not entirely resolved and removed in the text of tradition. Even in this case, the removed cannot but inhabit, perhaps secretly, like a specter, *unheimlich*, the building grounded on its removal. Deconstruction will thus amount to a double gesture: detecting the traces of the removed writing within the building constructed on its removal, at the same time as beginning to practice another writing, a writing able to account for those possibilities of meaning implicit in the notion of arche-writing and removed by phonetico-alphabetic writing.

Before examining in greater detail what deconstruction is, we should understand the relevance of this double gesture that Derrida seems to associate with the *sense* of deconstruction, that is, not only to its signification but also to its orientation, task, to-come:

> The end of linear writing is indeed the end of the book, even if, even today, it is within the form of a book that new writings—literary or theoretical—allow themselves to be, for better or for worse, encased. It is less a question of confiding new writings to the envelope of a book than of finally reading what wrote itself between the lines in the volumes. That is why, beginning to write without the line, one begins also to reread past writing according to a different organization of space. If today the problem of reading occupies the forefront of science, it is because of this

suspense between two ages of writing. Because we are beginning to write, to write differently, we must reread differently.[4]

We must write otherwise, and to do this we must read otherwise the text inherited from the tradition. In particular, reading otherwise means reading by taking into account the spatial organization of the texts of the tradition—testing for instance the grip of the linear structure, which is by its essence archeo-teleological, with respect to the concrete construction of the text. Therefore, writing otherwise means writing according to a different organization of space through the breaches that have already fractured the texts of the tradition. At this point I can reformulate my hypothesis in a clearer way: the architecture of deconstruction, as a writing of space, as a mode of spacing, should be a practical articulation of the possibilities of elaboration of sense implicit in arche-writing and removed within the model of phonetico-alphabetic writing. To support this hypothesis, it is worth recalling Derrida's reply to architects when asked about the architecture of deconstruction:

> I must confess, I have no model. If there is one, I have the feeling my architectural model must be read in my text. So *Glas* or *La carte postale* is . . . an organization of space. *Glas* for instance is not only a book on the theme of the column in Hegel. It is in itself an architecture, an architectural artifact. That is my only answer, a very modest one. I have the feeling that my repressed desire for music and architecture comes back through my writing and what interests me in writing, beside the content or the thesis, is the form, the spatial form . . . I am unable to draw out of my text an architectural model. But if there is one, well read the text. Inhabit the text if you can.[5]

Let us cross this threshold.

From writing to arche-writing

In a conversation with Peter Eisenman, probably in the latest stage of their difficult collaboration, Derrida is even more explicit regarding the relation between arche-writing and architectural writing:

> What interested me most, in my attempt to transform the concept of writing, was a writing able to escape the analogy with the writing of the book. I was thinking about a writing freed from the model of the book, a non- or pre-discursive writing. I was interested in traces and spacing that were not yet a discourse but make discursivity possible. At this stage of writing, writing does not consist in representing speech or a discourse, but in traits of spacing and thus is closer to the production of architectural drawing. I mean the drawing of the architect who organizes the space even before speaking and marks traits in the space that can be considered writing. Therefore, *Writing architecture* means writing by drawing, spacing out; this architecture is no longer the object of writing, it is tracing itself [*tracement*]. It is tracing, spacing, opening the space, *frayer*, you would say in French.[6]

This passage is essential. On the one hand, it evidently refers to the aforementioned passage from *Of Grammatology*, on the other hand, it further elaborates the articulation between arche-writing and architectural writing, the definition of the architecture of deconstruction as the writing of space, as a modality of spacing. We must escape the model of the book, not so much its concrete structure as the model embodied by the book:

> The good writing has therefore always been comprehended. Comprehended as that which had to be comprehended: within a nature or a natural law,

created or not, but first thought within an eternal presence. Comprehended, therefore, within a totality, and enveloped in a volume or a book. The idea of the book is the idea of a totality, finite or infinite, of the signifier; this totality of the signifier cannot be a totality, unless a totality constituted by the signified preexists it, supervises its inscriptions and its signs, and is independent of it in its ideality. The idea of the book, which always refers to a natural totality, is profoundly alien to the sense of writing. It is the encyclopedic protection of theology and of logocentrism against the disruption of writing, against its aphoristic energy, and, as I shall specify later, against difference in general. If I distinguish the text from the book, I shall say that the destruction of the book, as it is now under way in all domains, denudes the surface of the text. That necessary violence responds to a violence that was no less necessary.[7]

We must write otherwise, according to other possibilities of spacing. A writing that, according to Derrida, can be found precisely in architectural writing, as it is evidently understood otherwise, and thus set free from the link that binds it to metaphysics. A "nondiscursive" or "prediscursive" writing. Given that arche-writing is the condition of possibility of experience and thus of the elaboration of meaning in general, this writing should build up a concrete articulation of these conditions and in particular of those possibilities of meaning that have been removed by our tradition through the subordination of writing to speech and the subordination of writing to the linear ideal of phonetico-alphabetic writing. Within our tradition, this ideal is also the *telos* that has forced us to interpret all historical forms of writing different from phonetico-alphabetic writing as moments of a long maturation toward the *telos* of the phonetico-alphabetic accomplishment, rather than as forms appropriate to the demands made by the sense of a determinate culture and thus as possible concrete articulations of arche-writing. There have been other forms of writing before phonetico-alphabetic writing, and the traces of these kinds of writing still inhabit phonetico-alphabetic writing, as it has never fully developed according to its ideal. Therefore, Derrida is interested in architectural writing as the writing of deconstruction can be elaborated through it, that is, writing as an organization of space, as a multidimensional modality of spacing. If not through architecture, where has a multidimensional writing ever been practiced? Architectural writing is able to articulate geometric and mathematical notation, perspectival drawing and multiple reference systems, computer graphics, diagrams, photography, spectrography (which detects the physical nature of sites and materials as well as the anthropic presence), tridimensional models, and so on. I will discuss this issue later, by indulging for a moment in an apparently paradoxical affirmation from Derrida's "No (Point of) Madness—Maintaining Architecture": the architecture of deconstruction must have no meaning. In view of a writing of space, we must wrest architecture away from the subordination that it shares with writing, at a different level but with analogous effects. We must set architecture free from the role of a simple instrument of the exterior representation of a supposedly autonomous and independent meaning, which would not need architecture to be produced:

> The concept of architecture is itself an inhabited *constructum*, a legacy that understands us even before we try to think it. Certain invariants remain through all the mutations of architecture. Impassable, imperturbable, an axiomatic traverses the whole history of architecture. An axiomatic, that is to say, an organized whole of fundamental and always presupposed evaluations. This hierarchy has fixed itself in stone; henceforth, it informs the entirety of social space. What are these invariants? I will distinguish four, the slightly artificial charter of four traits, let

us say, rather, of four points. They translate one and the same postulate: *architecture must have a meaning*, it must *present* this meaning, and hence *signify*. The signifying or symbolic value of this meaning must command the structure and syntax, the form and function of architecture. It must command it *from the outside*, according to a principle (*archē*), a grounding or foundation, a transcendence or finality (*telos*) whose locations are not themselves architectural.[8]

Besides historical variations, which are certainly meaningful, here Derrida synthetically refers to the conception of signification elaborated throughout our tradition. On the one hand, there is a meaning produced within the soul, subjectivity, or consciousness; on the other hand, a representation of this meaning is required to communicate and transmit it to others. A signifier is required whose material substance can be varying, more or less opaque, more or less resistant, with respect to the transparent expression of a signification. It is for this reason that, from Plato to Hegel, until Saussure and beyond, speech is considered as the proper element of the immediate and transparent transmission of a signification while writing facilitates the dispersion of the latter by dissociating the latter from its production and emission. Within our tradition, according to this axiomatic, and by virtue of its materiality, architecture does not only undergo the treatment reserved to writing but also constitutes the privileged example of the imposition of this axiomatic as the evidence itself, at least in its privileged moment: Hegelian philosophy, with its semiology, which was studied by Derrida in an important essay entitled "The Pit and the Pyramid." We can find in this essay another trace of Derrida's elaboration of the law of the *oikos*. We may even recognize here the first arrangement of elements that will serve the deconstruction of architecture and, in particular, the first appearance of the question of *maintenance* as well as of the subordination of architecture to the metaphysical structure of sign. Derrida focuses on the example that Hegel takes up to determine the status of the sign through the opposition inside/outside that articulates the most general opposition of the system: spirit/matter. The example is borrowed from architecture, namely, the Egyptian pyramid. It allows Hegel to affirm that the external form of the signifier merely indicates the presence of a signification retained within itself and thus the absolute independence of the spiritual nature of the internal signification from the material form by means of which it manifests itself:

> Hegel knew that this proper and animated body of the signifier was also a *tomb*. The association *sōma/sēma* is also at work in this semiology, which is in no way surprising. The tomb is the life of the body as the sign of death, the body as the other of the soul, the other of the animate psyche, of the living breath. But the tomb also shelters, maintains in reserve, capitalizes on life by marking that life continues elsewhere. The family crypt: *oikēsis*. It consecrates the disappearance of life by attesting to the perseverance of life. Thus, the tomb also shelters life from death. It *warns* the soul of possible death, warns (of) death of the soul, turns away (from) death. This double warning function belongs to the funerary monument. The body of the sign becomes the monument in which the soul will be enclosed, preserved, maintained (*maintenue*), kept in maintenance (*maintenance*), present, signified. At the heart of this monument the soul keeps itself alive, but it needs the monument only to the extent that it is exposed—to death—in its living relation to its own body. It was indeed necessary for death to be at work—the *Phenomenology of Spirit* describes the work of death—for a monument to come to retain and protect the life of the soul by signifying it. The sign—the monument-of-life-in-death, the monument-of-death-in-life, the sepulcher of a soul

or of an embalmed proper body, the height conserving in its depth the hegemony of the soul resisting time, the hard text of stones covered with inscription—is the *pyramid*.[9]

Here Derrida reconstructs the structure of what he will designate as the "the law of the *oikos*." He indicates the trace that we should follow to go back to its foundation on Greek soil. The tomb plays for death the same role as the house plays for life: it protects, guards, and capitalizes what is proper of the *oikos*, keeps its stability and permanence—identity and presence—for the time to come, beyond the individual and contingent life of its components. The Greek language keeps the sense of this analogy in the term *oikēsis*, for instance, in Sophocles's *Antigone*, an important source for the Hegelian determination of the family, which Derrida will explore extensively in *Glas*: "O tomb! O bridal bedchamber! O deep / Cave of a dwelling-place (*oikēsis*), under guard forever."[10] However, in "The Pit and the Pyramid" there is an even more precise reference, and in this case it refers to the Greek soil and in particular to Plato and the mythico-religious heritage that influences the foundation of metaphysics. Indeed, where Derrida finds in the association *sōma/sēma*, the obscure ground from which Hegelian semiology draws, he refers to Plato (as confirmed by the terminology adopted to translate Hegelian conceptuality: spirit/matter, soul/body). The asterisk inscribed in the aforementioned passage marks the presence of a note. Here Derrida quotes a long passage from the *Cratylus* (400b–c) and refers to an analogous text from the *Gorgias* (493a):

Socrates: you mean "body (*sōma*)"?—Hermogenes: yes.—Soc.: I think this admits of many explanations, if a little, even very little, change is made; for some say it is the *tomb* (*sēma*) of the soul, their notion being that the soul is buried in present life; and again, because by its means the soul gives any signs which it gives (*sēmainei ha an sēmainēi nē psukhēi*), it is for

> this also properly called "sign" (*sēma*). But I think it most likely that the Orphic poets gave this name, with the Idea that the soul is undergoing punishment for something; they think it has the body for an enclosure to keep it safe, like a prison, and this is, as the name itself denotes, the safe (*sōma*, prison) for the soul until the penalty is paid, and not even a letter needs to be changed.[11]

Therefore, according to the axiomatic that governs our conception of the sign and the processes of signification, architecture would be bound to lose. Its matter is the most opaque, the most resistant to the transparent transmission of a supposedly transparent signification. For Derrida, however, this axiomatic does not exhaust the possibility of the elaboration of meaning. Above all, this axiomatic does not work: on the one hand, it is never carried out according to this ideal of the transparency of meaning. On the other hand, to found this ideal it had to remove the very possibility of the elaboration of meaning, which is quite irreducible, and it is for this nonempirical reason that this axiomatic is never realized according to its ideal. The spacing of meaning that characterizes writing as well as every system of notation is not just a necessity of an empirical kind—the transmission of meaning beyond the spatial and temporal limits inherent to personal allocution—but is, above all, an irreducible condition of experience and thus of any production of meaning. Therefore, spacing has already been at work within the single consciousness and constitutes the later as such. Derrida has explained this since his first writings on Husserl. In *Of Grammatology*, he calls it "arche-writing."

Détour. From arche-writing to mythography

> If the trace, arche-phenomenon of "memory," which must be thought before the opposition of nature and culture, animality and humanity, and so on, belongs

to the very movement of signification, then signification is a priori written, whether inscribed or not, in one form or another, in a "sensible" and "spatial" element that is called "exterior." Arche-writing, at first the possibility of the spoken word, then of the "graphie" in the narrow sense, the birthplace of "usurpation," denounced from Plato to Saussure, this trace is the opening of the first exteriority in general, the enigmatic relationship of the living to its other and of an inside to an outside: spacing. The outside, "spatial" and "objective" exteriority that we believe we know as the most familiar thing in the world, as familiarity itself, would not appear without the *gramme*, without différance as temporalization, without the nonpresence of the other inscribed within the sense of the present, without the relationship with death as the concrete structure of the living present.[12]

What, finally, is arche-writing? The understanding of the genesis and structure of memory as the irreducible condition of experience is at stake. If we are unable to produce and keep a trace that refers to our lived experience, we could not refer to (that is, recollect) the latter in another moment of our own experience and consequently there would be no experience. Now, for this recognition to be possible, it is required that a trace be different from the experience to which it refers, so long as this experience is present and lively but transitory. This entails that, in order to fix a moment in the temporal flow of our experience our memory must space out, it provides the support for the inscription of those traces that refer to the punctual present of experience while differentiating from the latter. Therefore, the spacing of meaning that characterizes every system of graphic marking is not only a necessity of empirical nature—communication—but above all an irreducible condition of experience and thus of every production of meaning. The retention of the trace of experience in the individual consciousness is always affected by an irreducible detachment from the immediate and living present of intuition, since only this detachment allows consciousness to recognize the "same" in a reference to come, which is absolutely other than the "living present" of its supposedly originary production. The spacing out that grants the iteration of the trace has already been at work within the single consciousness and constitutes it as such:

> Before the "same" is recognized and communicated among several individuals, it is recognized and communicated within the individual consciousness: after quick and transitory evidence, after a finite and passive retention vanishes, its sense can be re-produced as the "same" in the act of recollection; its sense has not returned to nothingness. In this *coincidence of identity*, *ideality* is announced as such and in general in an egological subject. . . . Thus, before being the ideality of an identical object for other subjects, sense is this ideality for *other* moments of the same subject in a certain way, therefore, intersubjectivity is first the non-empirical relation of Ego to Ego, of my present to other presents as such; i.e., as others and as presents (as past presents). Intersubjectivity is the relation of an absolute origin to other absolute origins, which are always my own, despite their radical alterity. Thanks to this circulation of primordial absolutes, the *same* thing can be thought through absolutely other moments and acts.[13]

Our memory thus works as a writing that precedes any recourse to an empirical writing.[14] The consequences of this argument are enormous, at least for Derrida. I will limit myself to recalling some of them: it is only from this possibility of spacing out, of the iterable trace that ipseity differentiates itself from the environment, from alterity in general, like a self from the others, an inside from an outside, an inside that, however, is necessarily open onto the outside that constitutes it by virtue of spacing out. There is a distinction, a differential relation but not an opposition between terms. Therefore, spacing out is what differentiates at the same time as it puts into relation. Differentiation/relation precede and constitute opposite terms so that they cannot ever be constituted by themselves outside this differentiation/relation nor dominate and appropriate it. From this perspective, what is removed, through the subordination of writing to the linear phonetico-alphabetic ideal, is precisely the potential implicit in spacing out and thus in arche-writing as a condition of experience. It is precisely from this potential that Derrida proposes to draw again in *Of Grammatology*. He takes into account the possibility of "grammatology as a positive science,"[15] a science that should account for the different forms of the elaboration of meaning as the concrete articulations of the arche-writing of experience:

> When does writing begin? Where and when does the trace, writing in general, common root of speech and writing, narrow itself down into "writing" in the colloquial sense? Where and when does one pass from one writing to another, from writing in general to writing in the narrow sense, from the trace to the *graphie*, from one graphic system to another, and, in the field of a graphic code, from one graphic discourse to another, etc.?[16]

In particular, Derrida highlights the improvements and limits of the sciences of writing. On the one hand, they made explicit that phonetico-alphabetic writing merely constitutes an epoch of our history, in particular, of Western history: there were and have been other forms of writing. On the other hand, however, these stories of writing meet a precise limit: the typological classifications that build up the research field are unable to account for more complex and articulated realities, which are allergic to rigid classifications: "The greatest difficulty was already to conceive, in a manner at once historical and systematic, the organized cohabitation, within the same graphic code, of figurative, symbolic, abstract, and phonetic elements."[17]

If it is true that the phonetico-alphabetic writing must necessarily recur to graphic marking without phonic correspondence, however, massively nonphonetic writing such as Chinese writing displays phonetic elements. Other writings, such as the Egyptian and Aztec ones, are at once, even in the same single element, symbolic, abstract, and phonetic.[18] This multidimensionality of writing and thus of the elaboration of meaning is the most general condition of the concrete elaboration of arche-writing. Simultaneously, multidimensionality is precisely what is removed in the age of phonetico-alphabetic writing, although the latter is never fully erased. This multidimensional writing is designated by Derrida as "mythogram," a term and concept borrowed from Leroi-Gourhan:

> Writing in the narrow sense—and phonetic writing above all—is rooted in a past of nonlinear writing. It had to be defeated, and here one can speak, if one wishes, of technical success; it assured a greater security and greater possibilities of capitalization in a dangerous and anguishing world. But that was not done *one single time*. A war was declared, and a suppression of all that resisted linearization was installed. And first of what Leroi-Gourhan calls the "mythogram," a writing that spells its symbols pluri-dimensionally; there the meaning is not subjected to successivity, to the order of a logical time, or to the irreversible temporality of sound. This pluri-dimensionality does not paralyze history within simultaneity, it corresponds to another level of historical experience, and one may just as well consider, conversely, linear thought as a reduction of history.[19]

The writing of deconstruction must be multidimensional: it must draw together phonetic, graphic, symbolic, concrete, and abstract elements, without subordinating them to a pre-constituted hierarchy that would be superior and external to spacing. This does not mean that this writing is accidental, nor that it aims to blur the borders between figurative arts, literature, and writing. We should rather think of this writing as the elaboration of meaning able to respond to the multidimensionality of experience, of an experience that is differentiated in itself (affection, sensation, intuition, perception, memory, desire, gesture, knowledge, ideality, etc.). Our tradition has impoverished this experience since the time when the former subordinated the latter to the order of presence and thus within the horizon of the appropriation of the otherness of the other in general. Furthermore, deconstruction must wrest the multidimensionality of meaning away from the appropriation of those forces—already at work in the sixties, according to Derrida—that have been interested in neutralizing its effects within the limits of an age or in reducing it to a mere instrument for the transmission of a preconstituted signification.

From mythography to architecture

The aforementioned passage from *Of Grammatology* is followed by the passage that I mentioned at the beginning, the passage in which Derrida announces the end of the book and the urgency of another writing/reading for deconstruction, a writing/reading able to account for the irreducible spacing of meaning. This passage ends as follows:

> What is thought today cannot be written according to the line and the book, except by imitating the operation implicit in teaching modern mathematics with an abacus. This inadequation is not *modern*, but it is exposed today better than ever before. The access to pluridimensionality and to a delinearized temporality is not a simple regression toward the "mythogram"; on the contrary, it makes all the rationality subjected to the linear model appear as another form and another age of mythography. The meta-rationality or the

meta-scientificity which are thus announced within the meditation upon writing can therefore be no more shut up within a science of man than conform to the traditional idea of science. In one and the same gesture, they leave *man*, science, and the line behind.[20]

It is the possibility of this mythography, the access to this multidimensional writing, that Derrida is seeking through deconstruction and, in particular, the architecture of deconstruction. He practices this writing of space in some of his texts—think of *Glas*—that we should read as architecture, in the evidently transformed meaning of architectural writing, according to this process of transformation of which, I hope, I have highlighted at least the necessity, the bases, and the effects. Derrida finds this transformation already at work in Bernard Tschumi's writing:

> The invention here consists in crossing the architectural motif with what is most singular and most closely competing in other writings, which are themselves drawn into the said madness, in its plural, that of photographic, cinematographic, choreographic, and even mythographic writing. As *The Manhattan Transcripts* demonstrated (the same is true, though in a different way, of La Villette), a narrative montage of great complexity outwardly explodes the narrative that mythologies contracted or effaced in the hieratic presence of the monument "for memory." An architectural writing interprets (in the Nietzschean sense of active, productive, violent, transformative interpretation) events that are *marked* by photography or cinematography. Marked: provoked, determined *or* transcribed, captured, in any case always mobilized in a scenography of passage (transference, translation, transgression from one place to another, from a place of writing to another, graft, hybridization). Neither architecture nor anarchitecture:

transarchitecture. It comes to terms with the event; it no longer offers its work to users, believers, or dwellers, to contemplators, aesthetes, or consumers. Instead, it calls on the other to *invent*, in turn, the event, to sign, consign, or *countersign*: advanced by an advance made to the other—and *maintaining* architecture, *now* architecture.[21]

It is neither by chance nor by a literary caprice that Tschumi's writing is interpreted here as a mythography.

5

WRITING SPACE

Between Tschumi and Derrida

IN *OF GRAMMATOLOGY*, WHICH WE CAN READ AS THE theoretical matrix of deconstruction, Derrida aimed to show that the spacing of meaning that characterizes every system of graphic notation is not only a necessity of an empirical order—registration and transmission. Above all, it is the irreducible condition of experience and thus of any production of meaning. Therefore, spacing has already been at work from within the single consciousness and constitutes it as such. In particular, Derrida demonstrates that our memory—the irreducible condition of the constitution of experience and thus of every form of ipseity—works precisely as a writing, before any recourse to an empirical writing. This is why he defines this condition as arche-writing:

> If the trace, arche-phenomenon of "memory," which must be thought before the opposition of nature and culture, animality and humanity, etc., belongs to the very movement of signification, then signification is a priori written, whether inscribed or not, in one form or another, in a "sensible" and "spatial" element that is called "exterior." Arche-writing, at first the possibility of the spoken word, then of the "graphie" in the narrow sense, the birthplace of "usurpation," denounced from Plato to Saussure, this trace is the opening of the first exteriority in general, the enigmatic

relationship of the living to its other and of an inside to an outside: spacing.¹

It is from this perspective that all forms of the elaboration of the sense of experience—from memory to verbal language, from writing to the most sophisticated systems of notation—constitute concrete articulations of arche-writing. That is, of spacing as the elaboration of those traces able to produce meaning through their differential articulation, through a network of references that constitutes experience as a tissue of traces and not as the horizon of intentional projections, of already constituted meanings. It is this potential of meaning implicit in the spacing of experience that must be removed in the name of an ipseity that would be able to master the territory of experience in full autonomy with respect to an alterity to which it would be related only secondarily. According to Derrida, deconstruction must liberate the spacing of meaning from the removal that it has undergone throughout our tradition at the same time as it must begin to practice another writing. By this I mean a writing that is no longer subordinated to the phonetico-alphabetic ideal and thus to the linear model that links the elaboration of meaning to an archeo-teleological development, so as to secure the path of meaning from an origin to a presupposed end behind or beyond the space in which meaning is inscribed:

> The end of linear writing is indeed the end of the book, even if, even today, it is within the form of a book that new writings—literary or theoretical—allow themselves to be, for better or for worse, encased. It is less a question of confiding new writings to the envelope of a book than of finally reading what wrote itself between the lines in the volumes. That is why, beginning to write without the line, one begins also to reread past writing according to a different organization of space. If today the problem of reading

occupies the forefront of science, it is because of this suspense between two ages of writing. Because we are beginning to write, to write differently, we must reread differently.[2]

The stakes of another writing are evidently very high. I will limit myself to noting that this writing must write according to another organization of space—in particular, it must be a multidimensional writing. Derrida also calls it *mythography*, borrowing the term, and not only the term, from Leroi-Gourhan:

> Writing in the narrow sense—and phonetic writing above all—is rooted in a past of nonlinear writing. It had to be defeated, and here one can speak, if one wishes, of technical success; it assured a greater security and greater possibilities of capitalization in a dangerous and anguishing world. But that was not done *one single time*. A war was declared, and a suppression of all that resisted linearization was installed. And first of what Leroi-Gourhan calls the "mythogram," a writing that spells its symbols pluri-dimensionally; there the meaning is not subjected to successivity, to the order of a logical time, or to the irreversible temporality of sound.[3]

The writing of deconstruction must be multidimensional: it must recuperate the structural principle and potentiality of *mythography* that precedes the domination of phonetico-alphabetic writing, without returning to those primitive forms of writing. Rather, it must interweave systems of phonetic, graphic, symbolic, concrete, and abstract notations, without subordinating them, according to a preestablished hierarchy, to a sovereign meaning, a meaning that would be superior and external with respect to the spacing in which these systems are inscribed and articulated. This does not mean that it would occur by chance, but in view of an elaboration of meaning able to respond to the multidimensionality of experience, which is, in itself, differentiated and multilayered.

From mythography to architecture (A/R)

What is at stake in this other writing is thus the possibility of the elaboration of the meaning of our experience. It is precisely at this point that architecture enters the stage. Rather, architecture has always already been involved, as it is the organization of space, namely, writing. Derrida was interested in architectural writing precisely because it allowed him to elaborate a writing understood as the organization of space, as the multidimensional modality of spacing. Where, if not in architecture, has multidimensional writing always been practiced?

However, the hierarchy that ties architectural writing to the presentation of a signification, of a superior and external meaning, is still to be deconstructed. Architecture must be still liberated from the empire of meaning, which does not entail imagining a meaningless architecture but thinking other possibilities of meaning through architectural writing. It is this deconstruction and multidimensional elaboration of meaning that Derrida sees to come through Tschumi's work: "the imminence of what is happening to us now [*de ce qui nous arrive maintenant*] announces not only an architectural event [*événement*]: rather a writing of space, a mode of spacing that makes a place for the event [*un mode d'espacement qui fait sa place à l'événement*]."[4]

The architecture of deconstruction must be the writing of space and precisely of a way of spacing, of the archewriting of experience. This possibility seems to take place in Tschumi's work. It is not by chance that Derrida designates architectural writing as "mythography." He understands this writing without aiming to explain a supposedly unique meaning:[5] "The invention here consists in crossing the architectural motif with what is most singular and most closely competing in other writings, which are themselves drawn into the said madness, in its plural, that of photographic, cinematographic, choreographic, and even mythographic writing."[6]

Beyond the occurrence of the term, it is evident that Derrida finds in Tschumi's architectural writing the traits of the multidimensional writing described in *Of Grammatology*, not only because, as we will see, it displays a weave of multiple systems of notation, but above all, because this weave ties together notation systems that refer to different and concomitant types of experience: (a) architectural writing, whose system of representation is linked to the realization of a finished product, according to points of view established by convention; (b) photographic writing, which can comply with conventional points of view as well as with others in which the singularity of the experience of the sight intervenes; (c) cinematographic writing, in which the duplicity of the point of view (conventional/singular) is being developed through movement and thus by inscribing a kinesthetic dimension within the space of a stable architectural presence; (d) choreographic writing able to register, elaborate, and reproduce the traces of this kinesthetic dimension and thus to wrest the corporeal experience of space away from contingency and abstraction, to which architectural planning is commonly bound. The inscribed traces no longer refer to meanings presupposed in a homogeneous space; they produce differential relations between horizons of meaning that are habitually considered opposed and noncompatible: the objectivity of a constituted space and the singularity of the experience inscribed in it, the stable presence of the architectural product and the aleatory corporeal movements that can be conditioned by the constituted space or contribute to the constitution of a still undetermined space. But what counts more is that, for Derrida, these different notation systems are not bound to the realization of a preestablished project. On the contrary, they can be joined in frameworks, assemblages, and different combinations that are able to offer different planning and constructive solutions. Therefore, they are liable to diverse interpretations that are also competitive and, above all, the series of which in principle resists closure, saturation, and the obligation of a unique meaning. This does not mean affirming the equivalence of any solution/interpretation—according to an old, postmodernist cliché—but, rather, showing the multiplicity of possibilities that can intervene in the elaboration of architectural writing, at the same time as those possibilities that are removed in order to respect the obligations that the metaphysics of presence imposes on architecture, on interpretation, and above all on experience (the experience of architecture, of interpretation, and of alterity in general):

> As *The Manhattan Transcripts* demonstrated (the same is true, though in a different way, of La Villette), a narrative montage of great complexity outwardly explodes the narrative that mythologies contracted or effaced in the hieratic presence of the monument "for memory." An architectural writing interprets (in the Nietzschean sense of active, productive, violent, transformative interpretation) events that are *marked* by photography or cinematography. Marked: provoked, determined *or* transcribed, captured, in any case always mobilized in a scenography of passage (transference, translation, transgression from one place to another, from a place of writing to another, graft, hybridization). Neither architecture nor anarchitecture: transarchitecture.[7]

Therefore, Derrida finds in Tschumi the example of a writing that is able to render the dynamic process of signification as the elaboration and articulation of traces precisely by virtue of its spatial organization, a writing that not only does not suspend signification through a monumental reification but also, as a combinatorial possibility, remains a writing open to its own transformation. The sense of this writing is not preconstituted by its sovereign author but is the effect of the transformative interpretations of those who are thus invited to take part in its realization by interpreting given materials that, however, can be linked together in different ways, in view of different purposes, and for contrasting and antagonistic purposes. Those people are thus also invited to interpret themselves, among the aforementioned materials, that is, to interpret the role to which they are subjected: "It [transarchitecture] comes to terms with the event; it no longer offers its work to users, believers, or dwellers, to contemplators, aesthetes, or consumers. Instead, it calls on the other to *invent*, in turn, the event, to sign, consign, or *countersign*: advanced by an advance made to the other—and *maintaining* architecture, *now* architecture."[8] From this perspective, architectural writing could be open and give place to the irreducible alterity of the other, to the event that is always the to-come of an irreducible alterity, and thus to the possibility of a transformative interpretation that, being of the order of the possible, can also not take place, or, worse, can give place to any kind of misunderstanding, as well as to something unpredicted, such as the encounter with the other in its irreducible singularity, the very possibility of experience. For this writing, the possibility of becoming a work—of taking on other meanings—hinges on the other, on the decision of the other to engage itself and respond of/to the possibility opened by this writing/spacing. That is, of/to the opening of the space of experience brought back to the singular weave that stands behind a historically determinate cultural obligation:

> Such chance is not given to the inhabitant or the believer, the user or the architectural theorist, but to whoever engages, in turn, in architectural writing: without reservation, which implies an inventive reading, the unease of a whole culture, and the signature of the body. This body would no longer be content simply to *walk*, circulate, stroll around *in* a place or *on* paths, but would transform its elementary

motions by giving them place [*en leur donnant lieu*]; it would receive from this other spacing the invention of its gestures.⁹

Architectural writing. Between Derrida and Tschumi

At this point, to understand the meaning and implications of Derrida's interpretation, we must follow the traces and explore the space where they are inscribed and interwoven in order to elaborate possibilities of meaning that do not necessarily account for the supposed meaning of Tschumi's work but relaunch its opening. Above all, we must go through *The Manhattan Transcripts*,[10] where the reference to deconstruction is explicit. The latter are a set of drawings introduced by a text elaborated according to traditional criteria (6–11) and followed by a more complex text, built on two columns, like a storyboard, a script (xvii–xxviii). The right column is a vertical sequence of texts, divided into sub-sequences made of titled and numbered paragraphs. The left column is made of pictures, drawings, photograms, and diagrams that are differently related to the texts that flow along the other column. Therefore, it is a book that is constructed with quite varying graphic materials. Furthermore, it does not refer to a completed architectural work nor does it gather together the different stages of a design to be realized. It is rather a book of architecture with an explicit theoretical function:

> Books of architecture, as opposed to books *about* architecture, develop their own existence and logic. They are not directed at illustrating buildings or cities, but at searching for the ideas that underlie them. Inevitably, their content is given rhythm by the turning of pages, by the time and motion this suggests. The book may read as sequences, but they do not necessarily imply narratives. They can be theoretical projects, abstract endeavors aimed at both exploring the limits

of architectural knowledge and at giving readers access to particular forms of research.[11]

The drawings are grouped into four sequences entitled: MT1: THE PARK—MT2: THE STREET—MT3: THE TOWER—MT4: THE BLOCK. These sequences are constructed as a succession of cinematographic photograms.[12] Each sequence starts from one of the four urban elements that characterize Manhattan, and thus it develops through three planes, levels, or dimensions, by means of different notation systems, according to a device of assembly that is at once preestablished and open, and thus requires the constructive intervention of the observer/interpreter: "Three disjoined levels of 'reality' are presented simultaneously in the *Transcripts*. . . . At first, the respective importance of each level depends only on how each is interpreted by the viewer, since each level can always be seen against the background of another. In this sense, looking at the *Transcripts* also means constructing them."[13] The first plan represents the space, the second the movement, the third the event. Their intersection grants the possibility that what has always been excluded within a conventional architectural writing—experience as irreducibly singular—takes place.

> The original purpose of the tripartite mode of notation (events, movement, spaces) was to introduce the order of experience, the order of time—moments, intervals, sequences—for all inevitably intervene in the reading of the city. It also proceeded from a need to question the modes of representation generally used by architects: plans, sections, axonometries, perspectives. However precise and generative they have been, each implies a logical reduction of architectural thought to what can be shown, to the exclusion of the other concerns. They are caught in a sort of prison-house of architectural language, where "the limits of my language are the limits of my world."[14] Any attempt to go beyond such limits, to offer another reading of architecture, demanded the questioning of these conventions.[15]

To inscribe the singularity of experience within the space of architecture, it is necessary to deconstruct the traditional conventions that preside over architectural writing and subordinate it to the value of presence, allegedly objective and forever fixed, that is, "what can be displayed." These conventions affirm the sovereignty of the conventional point of view, that aims to be objective, abstract and disembodied, and through which multi-dimensional experience is merely denied, reduced to the rigidity of a disembodied look.[16] How does Tschumi plan to inscribe within architectural writing the singularity of experience, which is by itself of the order of the contingent, of the ineffable, of the aleatory? By deconstructing the traditional conventions of architectural writing through the use of different notation systems, by elaborating another writing of space without yielding to the modernist presumption that experience can be reduced to calculable and universal measurements, forever established:

> The movements—of crowds, dancers, fighters—recall the inevitable intrusion of bodies into architectural spaces, the intrusion of one order into another. The need to record accurately such confrontations, without falling into functionalist formulas, suggests precise forms of movement notation. An extension of drawing conventions or choreography, this notation attempts to eliminate the preconceived meaning given to particular actions in order to concentrate on their spatial effects: the movement of bodies in space.[17]

Let us observe the last sequence—THE BLOCK—in which deconstruction explicitly intervenes from the theoretical perspective adopted by Tschumi (see figures 1, 2, and 3). First level, space: some pictures of details from buildings in Manhattan are followed by a perspectival view of a street, which is reduced, according to the conventions of traditional architectural drawing, to the mere relief of volumes. A sequence of drawings follows, which reproduces the succession of cinematographic photograms. The architectural drawing is elaborated in a traditional fashion and

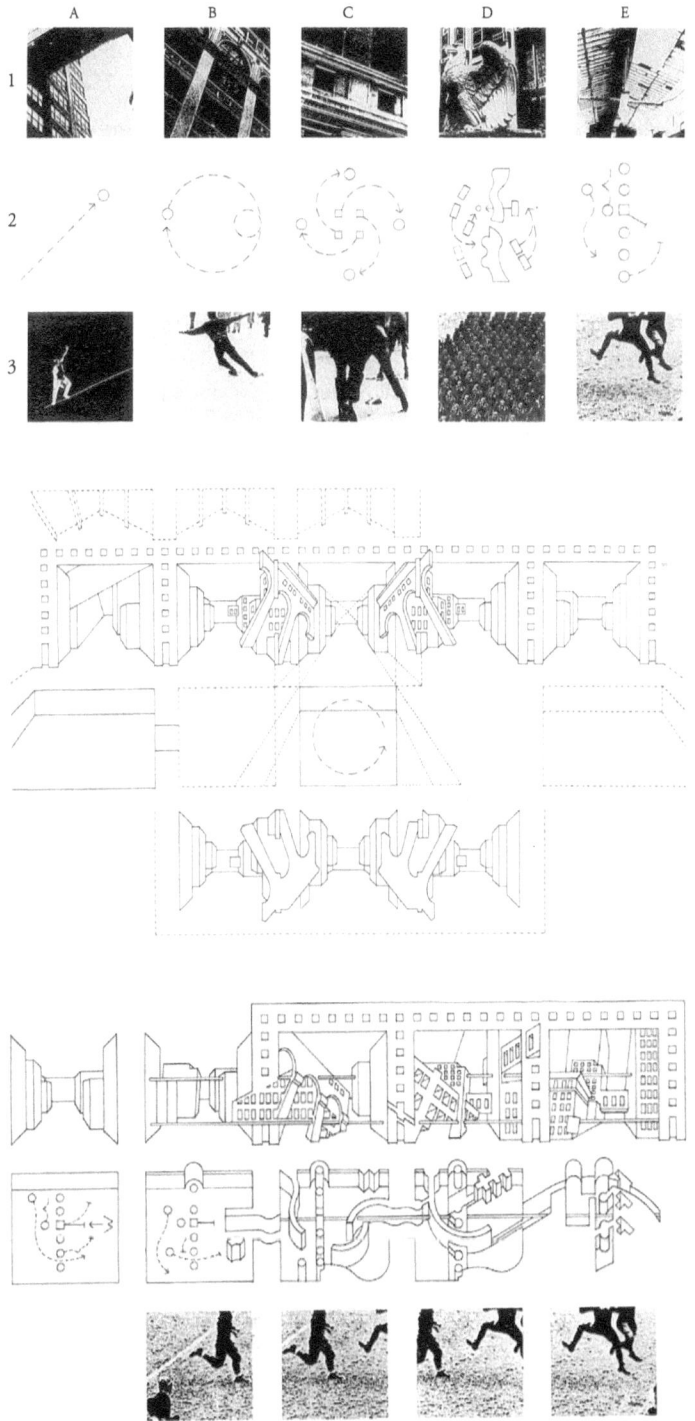

FIGURES 1, 2, 3   B. Tschumi, Manhattan Transcripts, pp. 46-48.

undergoes a set of transformations, as if the movie camera were in motion, a subjective movement that compresses and deforms the fixed, abstract, and conventional perspective of the initial drawing. Second level, movement: choreographic notation and the notation employed for football tactics record and reproduce the traces of movements dictated by different activities: acrobatics, dance, running, ice-skating, military marching. In the initial sequence, on the level of space that corresponds to perspectival drawing, there is no movement. At the perspectival center, we have a circular trajectory, without body, without the subject of movement, to indicate an abstract movement closed upon itself. As the sequence develops through the notation systems of movement, bodies are inscribed within space by trajectories that modify the abstract and linear geometries of perspectival drawing. Third level, the event: a series of pictures record and reproduce, through sequences or in the singular instant of the photographic act, the subjects of movements whose notation is given in the previous level: an acrobat who walks on a wire, runners, football players, a military parade, an ice-skater.

As the macro-sequence develops, it is possible to follow the gradual deformation of the traditional, architectural space, which results from different movements inserted in it produced, in turn, by the events that occur in real space. This is evident, in particular, in figure 4, where spatial deformation seems to reproduce the perception of the skater while she performs a pirouette, which is reproduced at the third level, the level of the event inscribed into space.

We cannot follow the three subsequences and their autonomous logic that aims to highlight the irreducible dissociation between "use, form, and social values. The non-coincidence between meaning and being, movement and space, man and object is the starting condition of the work."[18] These disjunctions affect the relationship between form and function, planning, and singular and contingent experience. Tschumi assigns a deconstructive bearing to the last scansion of the sequence, where the three levels intersect with one another in a complex weave, at the limits of the inextricable, of the chaotic, from which another space emerges: the architectural structure is deformed as if it were perceived in motion, as if, through their movement, some bodies traced material structures whose stability is however pushed to the limit of the possible, up to explode in fragments.

Tschumi aims to find a synthesis able to saturate and resolve the different disjunctions at play as well as to put to the test the combinatory possibilities that the disjunction provides, without concealing or removing their irreducibility or, thus, their uncanny and destructuring effect. Conversely, where it is pushed to the

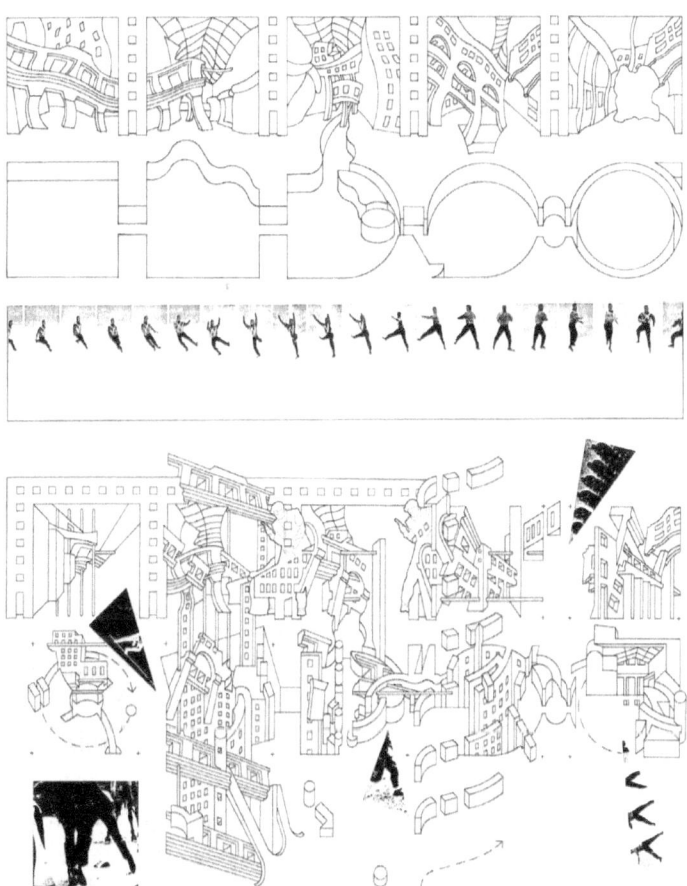

FIGURES 4, 5   *B. Tschumi, Manhattan Transcripts, pp. 50, 56.*

limits of the impossible, where it produces uncanny (*unheimlich*) effects, at the limits of the absence of sense, disjunction can show itself as the condition of possibility of architecture, understood as the rewriting of space. It can bring experience back to the event of spacing.[19]

> The last *Transcript* eliminates all that is inessential to the architecture of the city. Spaces, movements, events are contracted into the only fragments absolutely necessary to outline the overall structure. Since each frame is isolated from the next, architecture can begin to act as a series of surprises, a form of architectural *jump-cut*,[20] where space is carefully broken apart and then reassembled "at the limits." Thus space can follow space, not necessarily in the order normally expected, but in a series of dramatic revelations that can announce a new spatial structure. Devices such as the inversion of any additional space within a spatial sequence can change the meaning of the sequence as well as its impact on the experiencing subject (as in the noted Kuleshov experiment, where the same shot of the actor's impassive face is introduced in a variety of situations, and the audience reads different expressions in each successive juxtaposition). One last point: as opposed to logical transformation that proceeds from rules inherent in the nature of the object, the *Transcripts*' sequences often proceed from "subjective" modes. Although an objective rule is given arbitrarily (compression or superposition, for example), its implementation, articulation, and final form depend upon the person who applies the rule. In other words, such sequences cannot result from a simple cumulative process of logical transformations for which instructions can be given to anyone. In the same way, the pleasurable element of subjective arbitrariness enters the selection of endless images

of fighters or façades. (Rationally, only their essential characteristics need be defined.) Ultimately, the spatial relationships and physical dimensions of objects that change with each viewpoint are like movie shots from above that are intercut with those from below: reality is made infinitely malleable, so that emotive, dramatic, or poetic attributes can change and unfold.[21]

Beyond architecture

At this point, the congruence of the intersection between Tschumi's work and that of Derrida should be evident. The traces followed by Derrida do not saturate the space opened by Tschumi. There is no room for such a presumption in him, the classical presumption of philosophy, that of a preestablished meaning. Rather, he abides by the rules of transformative interpretation, to the elaboration of which he contributed through deconstruction, and to which Tschumi also dedicated his work. Derrida selected, combined, and relaunched the traces that interested him most. Sometimes, he turned them toward directions that Tschumi himself could not predict: architectural writing as the articulation of the spacing of experience, namely, arche-writing.[22] Therefore, *The Manhattan Transcripts* do not only constitute a merely theoretical work able to intervene in the design of real products according to trajectories that are not strictly direct and conventional (theory: planning: product), like in the case of the project of the Parc de La Villette in Paris.[23] Derrida reads *The Manhattan Transcripts* as a palimpsest of the project to which the essay "No (Point of) Madness—Maintaining Architecture" is dedicated, but also, as an architectural work (so does Tschumi). Architectural writing, understood as the writing of experience, as a writing of deconstruction, is already architecture: *mythography*. Here we can grasp its most radical, deconstructive bearing. The architecture of deconstruction must go through the material and conventional limits to which it has always been bound, being submitted to the *telos* and sovereignty of presence, of work/ sense. It must become a writing of space, a concrete and layered articulation of spacing, a writing of experience. Therefore,

> We can no longer give them [to the trace of this other writing] the value of documents, related illustrations, preparatory or pedagogical notes, the *hors-d'oeuvre*, in short, or the equivalent of theatrical rehearsals. No—and this is what seems most threatening to the architectural desire that still inhabits us. The immovable mass of stone, the vertical glass or metal plane that we had taken to be the very object of architecture (*die Sache selbst*, or "the real thing"), its undisplaceable effectivity is now apprehended in the voluminous text of multiple writings: superimpression of a *Wunderblock* . . . palimpsest grid, supersedimented textuality, bottomless stratigraphy that is mobile, light and abyssal, foliated, foliform.[24]

6

DIVERGENT TRACES

*Peter Eisenman as an
Interpreter of Deconstruction*

THE ENCOUNTER WITH PETER EISENMAN CONSTITUTES A decisive moment of Derrida's adventure in the territories of architecture. However, the initial empathy between them is severely put to the test during their collaboration for the La Villette park project and finally turns into irreducible discord. This discord becomes a polemic on the occasion of the congress (Critical Architecture and Contemporary Culture) held in Irvine, from October 26 to 28 in 1989.[1]

Eisenman, who promoted the congress alongside Derrida and J. Hillis Miller, was there. Derrida decided not to attend at the last minute, explaining that it was due to a "hold up in Paris" and instead sent a tape on which he had recorded his voice. However, the absence was not due, it seems, to contingent factors. Rather, it is likely that Derrida took advantage of the situation caused by his absence, in order to address to Eisenman a series of questions that concern precisely his *absence*, the role that this notion plays in Eisenman's theoretical work. Derrida invites Eisenman to engage with Benjamin's 1933 text "Erfharung und Armut" ("Experience and Poverty"), in which, under the threat of impending war, Benjamin sees in Nazi barbarism the absolute dissolution of the values of traditional culture, of the patrimony of the cumulative experiences of the past, and supposes that a new generation of Barbarians stands out on the horizon, a generation that can start again without respect for the past. They are artists who work as engineers

79

and thus oppose themselves to the traditional value of the aura and build up the radically new. Among them, Benjamin recalls cubists, such as Paul Klee, and modernist architects (especially, Adolf Loos).[2] However, before addressing Derrida's reference to Benjamin, we must first address the question of absence in Eisenman's work:

> Now don't worry, I'm not going to argue with you. And I'm not going to take advantage of my absence, not even to tell you that you perhaps believe in it, *absence*, too much. This reference to absence is perhaps one of the things (because there are others) that most troubled me in your discourse on architecture, and if that were my first question, you could perhaps profit from my absence to speak about it a little, about absence in general, about the role that this, "absence," will have been able to play at least in what you believed you could "say," if not "do," with your architecture. One could multiply examples, but I'm limiting myself to what you say about the presence of an absence in *Moving Arrows, Eros, and Other Errors*, which concerns Romeo's castle, "a palimpsest and a quarry," etc. This discourse on absence, or the presence of an absence, perplexes me, not only because it bypasses so many tricks, complications, traps that the "philosopher," especially if he is a bit of a dialectician, knows only too well and fears to find you caught up in it again, but also because it has authorized many religious interpretations, not to mention vaguely Judeo-transcendental ideologizations, of your work. I suspect a little that you liked and encouraged these interpretations even as you discretely denied it with a smile, which would make a misunderstanding a little more or a little less than a misunderstanding. My question has to do not only with absence or the presence of absence, but with God. Voilà, if I didn't come it isn't just because I'm tired and

overworked—held up in Paris—but precisely to have the opportunity to directly ask you a question about God that I would never have dared to do in Irvine if I had been present in person; instead, I'm glad that this question has come to you by way of this voice, that is to say on tape. The same question brings up others, a whole group of closely related questions, for example, at the risk to shocking you: whether it has to do with houses, museums, or university research laboratories, what distinguishes your architectural space from that of the temple, indeed of the synagogue (by this word I mean a Greek word expressing a Jewish concept)? Where will the break, the rupture have been in this respect, if there is one, if there was one, for you and other architects of this period with whom you feel yourself associated? I remain very perplexed about this subject; if I had been there, I would have been a difficult interlocutor.[3]

Beyond the irony of the passage, the discord is radical, and there is no doubt that its implications are amplified by Derrida's tone. He had never before expressed such a radical disagreement with Eisenman. What happened? Indeed, the collaboration for *Chora L Works* had already shown some divergences, but here Derrida seems to respond to an equally radical criticism that Eisenman had addressed to him in an interview published in the Spanish journal *Arquitectura*. Derrida mentions this criticism in the postscript of the letter, although he affirms that he did not read it before writing his letter:

P.S.1. This tape was recorded and this transcription finished when I read at the end of an interview (in a special edition of the Spanish magazine *Arquitectura* [270] devoted to "Deconstruction"—that's the title of the introduction) the following lines from you which were already anticipating my question: "I never talk about Deconstruction. Other people use that word because they are not architects. It is very difficult to talk about architecture in terms of deconstruction, because we are not talking about ruins or fragments. The term is too metaphorical and too literal for architecture. Deconstruction is dealing with architecture as a metaphor, and we are dealing with architecture as a reality . . . I believe Post-Structuralism is basically what I mean by Post-Modernism. In other words, Post-Modernism is Post-Structuralism in the widest sense of the word." I certainly believe that I would *not* subscribe to *any* one of these statements, to *any* one of these 7 sentences, neither to 1, nor 2, nor 3, nor 4, nor 5, nor 6, nor 7. But I cannot explain it here, and truly, I never talk much *about* deconstruction. Not spontaneously. If you wish, you could display 1, 2, 3, 4, 5, 6, 7 before the listener and try to convince them by refuting the contrary prepositions or you could leave out this p.s.[4]

We can imagine that Derrida decided to spell out his perplexities about Eisenman's theoretical work in response to the positions the latter expressed with regard to deconstruction. Indeed, if Derrida reads these affirmations as a sort of anticipated response to the questions raised in his letter, then it is evident that these questions concern how Eisenman understands deconstruction and the relationship between deconstruction and architecture. Given that he would not countersign any one of these affirmations, here Derrida argues that Eisenman did not understand deconstruction and that Eisenman's architecture, that is, his concept of architecture, has nothing to do with architecture of deconstruction and the deconstruction of architecture. First, Eisenman conceives of the "metaphysics of presence"—which, for Derrida, in the wake of Heidegger, constitutes the order of the discourse of the Western tradition—as a conceptual order that values real presence in its material and physical concreteness.

It is for this reason that, for Eisenman, the deconstruction of the metaphysics of presence cannot be taken literally but only metaphorically: because architecture realizes objects that must be physically present and last in time. On the other hand, how can we take seriously a theory that aims to dismantle the totality of what is present, physically present? The formula "metaphysics of presence" accounts for a conceptual system, whose first elaboration and formalization is traced back to Plato. This system governs and structures Western thought as a system of oppositions that is hierarchically organized and ordered according to the value of "presence," as it determines the being of beings, the meaning of what is, in terms of presence. This presence is in turn understood on the basis of the determination of the temporal present as an absolute instant that is independent of the becoming inherent in it. For this reason, the past and the future are mere declensions of presence, that is, past presence and future presence. For Plato, presence is what remains identical to itself and does not change. Therefore, given that what is physically present is also mutable as it is submitted to becoming, presence can only be an ideal determination and actual presence, that is, the meaning of what is actually and empirically present, is always related to the ideal presence of which it is a reflection or a copy. The meaning of empirical and actual presence, which is subjected to becoming, thus depends on ideal presence. The philosophical tradition declined the principle of presence in multiple ways and, in particular, in modernity, it determined the subject (or consciousness) as a self-presence and knowledge as an idealizing interiorization of what is merely present in experience. In particular, for Derrida, even Husserl's phenomenology is still dominated by the "metaphysics of presence," from which it wished to emancipate itself, precisely in the formulation of its "principle of principles," that is, the "living present" understood as the original source of the intentional acts of consciousness. Husserl believes that ideal knowledge can be traced back to the original intuition of the phenomenon of which there is knowledge, that is, to the living present of its intuition. Furthermore, he affirms that one can refer to the original intuition of the living present insofar as this present is not an absolute instant but encompasses its passing away into memory (primary retention) as well as its anticipation in the future (protention). In other words, for Husserl, in principle, one can always go back to the trace of this first, original impression that is sedimented in memory since this trace, which is the effect of retention, would be of the same nature as the living presence of which it carries the impression. The adventure of deconstruction begins precisely from the deconstruction of the "living present," which brings about a radically different conception of the trace, whose repercussions on our system of thought are enormous. I will try to summarize these effects. Given that the function of memory consists in making possible the reference of consciousness to something, in a moment that is different from the contingent moment of its immediate experience, it is structurally impossible that the mnesic trace be of the same order and nature as the living presence of its first occurrence. Rather, the mnesic trace, in order to work as such, must be structurally different from the living present of which it is supposed to be the trace (as if it were an impression). If things were not so, the mnesic trace would always be the trace of that living present, and I would be unable to acknowledge something that would occur in a living present different from the one of the first mnesic retention, as a second occurrence of the same present and not as a new impression in a new present. The mnesic trace functions as a written trace since both are essentially iterable. Therefore: 1) presence is not the origin but an effect of the trace, it is the trace that allows one to refer to something as present—including our consciousness—but that will always be present as a trace of something else and so forth; 2) there is no way to come back to the origin, to the originary presence of the trace in consciousness, nor it is possible to grasp in the trace the presence of its future occurrence; 3) the meaning, the signification of something, is neither given, nor internal to consciousness, independent from signs—traces—that allow for its transmission. It is an effect, which, in principle, is never definitive, of the network of references that traces elaborate into a text; this textual weave is what structures our consciousness (for this reason, Derrida calls it "arche-trace" and "arche-writing"):

> The living present springs forth out of its nonidentity with itself and from the possibility of the retentional trace. It is always already a trace. This trace cannot be thought out on the basis of a simple present whose life would be within itself; the self of the living present is primordially [*originairement*] a trace. The trace is not an attribute; we cannot say that the self of the living present "primordially is" it [*l'«est originairement»*]. Being-primordial [*l'être-originaire*] must be thought on the basis of the trace, and not the reverse. This arche-writing is at work at the origin of the sense.[5]

As we will see, Eisenman's double misreading depends on the fact that he does not understand how Derrida uses these terms. Let us return to Irvine, to the congress held in October 1989. Eisenman is floored. He does not reply immediately; he will do it later, in a letter published in the congress proceedings. He wishes to be equally ironic but, evidently, he feels as if he were refuted, if not mocked, by Derrida:

> After many months I find the time and the calm distance to reply to your extraordinary letter. I was pleased that you would take the time to write a letter of such energy and length, but also disturbed by what I perceived as an implied criticism in your words. At the symposium, I was also quite literally left speechless by your question, questions that I could not answer personally, questions that, indeed, must be directed to architecture. For a reply. Why was I so stunned,

so taken aback? Perhaps on first thought because I felt in your criticism a rejection of my work. However, after many rereadings, I no longer feel that same rush of defensiveness but rather a certain exhilaration, a certain sense of an *other* freedom. Why? Because in a way you are right. Perhaps what I do in architecture, in its aspirations and in its fabric, is not what could properly be called deconstruction. But things are not quite so simple: if my work is not something, then it raises questions as to what it is not! In attempting to interrogate what it is not, I will not give an answer to all your questions. Indeed, I do not think that the spirit of your letter was one of inquisition. Rather, your questions seem to outline a provocative framework for thinking about architecture.[6]

Eisenman attempts to divert attention away from himself, to interpret Derrida's questions as if they were posed to architecture in general and as if they were thus helpful to reflect upon architecture but also such that no architect can respond individually to them in an exhaustive way. However, he must defend himself from the criticism that is addressed directly to him. Finding Derrida's reference to God to be without relevance or seriousness, he responds to the question surrounding the presence/absence opposition that constitutes the conceptual grid of "Moving Arrows, Eros, and Other Errors" as well as *Chora L Works* (and of others of his works, as he recognizes in *Chora L Works*). As we will see, the question of God is not irrelevant but is structurally linked to that of the use of the presence/absence binary and to Benjamin's notion of aura that Eisenman refers to in his response:

> Yes, I am preoccupied by absence, but not in terms of this simple presence/absence dialectic, as you might think. For me as an architect each concept, as well as each object, has all that is *not* inscribed

within it as traces. I am preoccupied with absence, not voids or glass, because architecture, unlike language, is dominated by presence, by the real existence of the signified.[7]

Here we can detect some hints of Eisenman's misreading, especially apropos the trace, which is understood as something that "has" in itself what it is not. We start seeing that, for Eisenman, the trace is the trace of the past as well as of the future, since it retains what is absent, precisely the past and the future, like the living present of phenomenology. Furthermore, the presence that concerns Eisenman is not the concept of presence that is elaborated by metaphysics but the real presence of the architectural object, which for Eisenman constitutes the very meaning of the object itself. Therefore, he considers it necessary to untie this symbolic relation that has governed the theory and praxis of architecture up to modernism and to liberate the possibility of thinking architecture like a text whose elaboration includes different instances beside those that immediately derive from real presence (which constitutes the most evident condition of the architectural object):

> It is not that there is no possibility of deconstruction in architecture. But it cannot simply take issue with what you have called the metaphysics of presence. In my view, your deconstruction of the presence/absence dialectic is inadequate for architecture precisely because architecture is not a two-term but a three-term system. In architecture, there is another condition, which I call *presentness*—that is neither absence nor presence, form nor function, but rather an excessive condition between sign and being. As long as there is a strong bond between form and function, sign and being, the excess that contains the possibility of presentness will be repressed. The need to overcome presence, the need to supplement an architecture that will always

be and look like architecture, the need to break apart the strong bond between form and function, is what my architecture addresses. In its displacement of the traditional role of function, it does not deny that architecture must function, but rather suggests that architecture may also function without necessarily symbolizing that function.[8]

Derrida would not countersign a single word of this distinction between linguistic sign and symbol, nor would he subscribe to the definition of the sign as the unity of signifier and signified. Above all, affirming that a concept is not dialectical is not enough to make it so; one must demonstrate it and thus look at how the concepts that are employed function; one must verify that their construction is not dialectical, and on this point Eisenman seems to encounter great difficulties. He does not demonstrate that his recourse to the presence/absence binary is not dialectical and that it does not produce dialectical effects; nor does he explain the "presentness" on which everything, and thus his work as well as Derrida's misunderstanding, seems to hinge:

> Presentness is the possibility of another aura in architecture, one not in the sign or in being, but a third condition of betweenness. Neither nostalgic for meaning or presence nor dependent on them, this third nondialectical condition of space exists only in an excess that is more, or less, than the traditional hierarchical, Vitruvian precondition of form: structure, function, and beauty. This excess is not based on the tradition of the plenitude, but rather is the condition of possibility of presentness. This condition of aura is perhaps something that also remains unproblematized in your work, despite your protestations to the contrary. I believe that by virtue of architecture's unique relationship to presence,

to what I call presentness, it will always be a domain of aura. After all, aura is presence of absence, the possibility of a presentness of something else.⁹

But what does Eisenman understand by "presentness"? Above all, the term "presentness" indicates by itself an essence, the essence of presence, which determines the being present of something. However, if this essence must manifest through the play of absence/presence, how would we describe this play if not as dialectical? Let us look at this step more carefully: presentness should be a third condition of possibility of space that would exist only by exceeding the other two, presence and absence. This excess would grant the nondialecticity of this third condition. Now, given that an excess is sufficient to provide such a guarantee, Eisenman explains that this excess is the "condition of possibility of presentness." To summarize, he says: 1) presentness is a condition of possibility of space that is realized—exists—in excess between presence and absence at once; 2) this excess is the condition of possibility of presentness. Therefore, presentness is the condition of possibility of the excess that is the condition of possibility of presentness. Finally, tracing the meaning of presentness back to the excess and that of the excess back to presentness, Eisenman does not explain either of them. Indeed, he acknowledges that presentness cannot be explained by words, rational arguments, and images or drawings. One can only find it at play in the realized work or in the event of its realization, like the aura that emanates from a work:

> In the end, my architecture cannot be what it should be, but only what it can be. Only when you add one more reading of my work alongside yours of it in pictures and texts—that is, a reading in the event of a building—only there will you see the play between presence and presentness, only then will you know whether I have been faithful.¹⁰

Therefore, presentness is something in the order of the ineffable; it is like the aura of a work. But this reference to Benjamin's aura allows us to demonstrate that Derrida was right in criticizing Eisenman for his dialectic of presence and absence and finally for the inability to understand what metaphysics is. Let us take a step backward and return again to the aforementioned passage about the nondefinition of presentness and, in particular, to the second part that remains for us to examine:

> This excess is not based on the tradition of the plenitude, but rather is the condition of possibility of presentness. This condition of aura is perhaps something that also remains unproblematized in your work, despite your protestations to the contrary. I believe that by virtue of architecture's unique relationship to presence, to what I call presentness, it will always be a domain of aura. After all, aura is presence of absence, the possibility of a presentness of something else.

Therefore, this presentness would not be other than what makes possible the presentation of something that is not actually present within what is merely present. It is evident that Eisenman is here describing a dialectical relation to the extent that actual presence becomes the term through which is made present that which is absent and would remain as such if it were outside this relation (and thus simply in opposition to what is present). On the other hand, this is precisely the dialectic of the aura of the artwork as Benjamin describes it (without referring to Hegel), that is, as the secularized effect of the cultural value of the artwork and thus of the sacred function that was attributed to the simulacrum of god in the Greek temple (namely, the medium of manifestation of an otherwise inaccessible God):

> Originally, the embeddedness of an artwork in the context of tradition found expression in a cult. As we

know, the earliest artworks originated in the service of rituals—first magical, then religious. And it is highly significant that the artwork's auratic mode of existence is never entirely severed from its ritual function. In other words: *the unique value of the "authentic" work of art always has its basis in ritual.* This ritualistic basis, however mediated it may be, is still recognizable as secularized ritual in even the most profane forms of the cult of beauty.[11]

This is the reason why for Benjamin there is no renewal of the aura and its destruction is necessary if we want to liberate the field of art from its ritual and thus metaphysical legacy, if we want to promote the constructive principle advanced by the "new Barbarians." Benjamin evokes the latter in "Experience and Poverty," where they are said to destroy the past and work with what is available, with materials like iron and glass. Among them Benjamin places the architects of modernism. At this point, we understand Derrida's reference to Benjamin's text in his letter to Eisenman, and thus his reference to the question of God. Inviting Eisenman to engage with this text, Derrida asks him to take sides with respect to the question of the aura and its destruction. The fact that Eisenman responds by resorting to the aura in order to account for presentness as what interests him most turns out to confirm Derrida's perplexities. Indeed, Derrida had already expressed these perplexities during his discussion with Eisenman and his collaborators apropos the La Villette project. From the first session held on September 17, 1985, Derrida had spoken of his interest in architecture and in particular of the affinities between his work and that of Eisenman, but also of the metaphysical legacy that still anchors architecture. From this perspective, he had drawn attention to the danger of a metaphysical relapse implicit in the recourse to the dialectic of presence and absence, through which architecture would be caught up within its originally ritual function on this side of its secularization. As Benjamin observes, the secularization of the aura perpetuates its experiential structure—the ritual disposition with respect to the artwork and the auratic effect:

> I am excited and anxious. This is a very difficult situation for me, as I am operating in two foreign elements: architecture and the English language. When Bernard Tschumi first proposed this project to me, I was delighted but surprised, as I have no competence whatsoever in architecture. Nevertheless, I think I understand in a discursive, philosophical fashion what are you saying. When I read your texts and examined *Fin D'ou T Hou S*, I recognized many things: your critique of origin, anthropomorphism and aesthetics is consistent with a general deconstruction of architecture itself. Your work seems to propose an anti-architecture, or rather an anarchitecture, but of course this is not so simple, as what I do is antiarchitectural in the traditional sense of "anti." Yet I have always had the feeling of being an architect, in a way, when I am writing; I have a vague feeling that the form of whatever I am writing has an architectural dimension of the type you were describing. Anti-architecture, but with an architectural design—not a reference to architectural forms or schemes, but definitely something that has to deal with "building." The paradox, of course, is that on the face of it, architecture seems to have nothing to do with absence, in one of Heidegger's texts, he says that a temple is a place where God is present, but that implies that the temple is an empty place ready to receive God. It is the ultimate paradox of logocentrism. All other arts have a *telos* of representation, but architecture seems not to depend on it. So, because of its unique relationship to representation, architecture is more "present" than any other art, but at the same time, being the most "present," it is also the strongest reference to the opposite of presence, namely absence.[12]

The metaphysical bearing of architecture consists precisely in subjugating concrete presence to the manifestation of an absence that would determine the meaning of presence itself as if it were an ideal presence. Privileging absence means overturning the metaphysical hierarchy without affecting its conceptual structure. This is why Derrida goes on to advise Eisenman: "Well, you can strategically insist on absence as a disruption of the system of presence, but at a certain point you have to leave the theme of absence."[13] Eisenman neither embraces nor understands Derrida's advice, as he keeps on interpreting Derrida's notion of trace as the presence of an absence, where the absence determines what is present, which is anything but the traditional—and metaphysical—definition of sign: that which stands for something else. In particular, in *Chora L Works*, Eisenman gives the trace the meaning of impression, and thus the trace is not only understood as the actual presence of a past presence but still retains the latter insofar as it carries the impression of the past:

> Trace is a complex phenomenon—it is a suggestion of something before, or maybe the premonition of something after—the not yet present or the imagined past. . . . Chora introduced another possible conception of space as the distinction between trace and imprint. In my earlier projects, because there was no idea of receptacle, all of the marks were essentially traces, that is the residue of something that was formerly present. In the sense that the term is used here, what was formerly seen as a trace cannot be called an imprint.[14]

Within this framework, Eisenman's trace is analogous to the phenomenological one and far from the differential trace elaborated by Derrida. The situation is even clearer in "Moving Arrows, Eros, and Other Errors," and this is why Derrida's letter refers to this project and the related text. Above all, the procedure of *scaling* allows Eisenman to integrate within the project the function of the trace as the co-presence of the past and the future, according to the conception of trace that I defined as phenomenological and not deconstructive: "In *scaling, discontinuity* differentiates absence from void. Absence is either the trace of a previous presence, it contains *memory*; or the trace of a possible presence, it contains *immanence*."[15] Therefore, through scaling, the site of the project is not just absolutely given in its actual presence but is a trace, that is, the place in which the past as well as the possible future are co-present. Scaling thus integrates within the plan of the actual site what is actually absent, that is, the past and the future finally liberated from design conditions:

> By treating the site not simply as presence but as both palimpsest and a quarry, containing traces of both memory and immanence, "the site" can be thought of as non-static. Perhaps an analogy of the "non-static" would be useful. Consider the difference between a *moving arrow* and a still arrow. One only has to put one's hand in front of both to discover quickly the existence of a profound difference. Yet if a picture of each were taken and compared, they would be virtually indistinguishable. What distinguishes the moving arrow from the still one is that it contains where it has been and where it is going, i.e., it has a memory and an immanence that are not present to the observer of the photograph; they are essential *absences*. Theories of "the site" as present origin presume that the moving arrow and the still arrow are the same; they ignore the subtle but profound conditions of the presence of these absences.[16]

In conclusion, Eisenman himself affirms that scaling grounds a dialectic construction of the project:

> There are three important versions of the story of Romeo and Juliet which were taken as the basis of the

> "architectural program." Each narrative is characterized by three structural relationships, each having its own physical analogue: *division* (the separation of the lovers symbolized in physical form by the balcony of Juliet's house); *union* (the marriage of the lovers symbolized by the church); and their *dialectical relationship* (the togetherness and apartness of the lovers as symbolized in Juliet's tomb).... These are presented in three axonometric drawings, and scalings which are made by registering the three glasses in different superpositions. In each scaling there are present elements (in color), elements of memory (in grey), and elements of immanence (in white).[17]

At this point it is clear that the misunderstanding between Eisenman and Derrida derives from two divergent conceptions of the trace. On the one hand, Eisenman's trace, which we designated as phenomenological, allows us to go back to the presence of which it would be the direct effect and thus to prefigure a future presence. On the other hand, Derrida's trace results from the deconstruction of the phenomenological trace. According to Derrida, presence is not the origin of the trace but the local and transitory effect of the referential movement that the trace makes possible. It is evident that from this point Eisenman's and Derrida's paths cannot but diverge indefinitely.[18]

7

SPACING

The Architecture of Deconstruction

A SPECIAL ISSUE OF *PRECIS*, THE JOURNAL OF THE GRADUATE School of Architecture, Planning and Preservation of Columbia University, is dedicated to *The Culture of Fragments*.[1] Adopting a multidisciplinary perspective, it gathers together contributions from different fields (architects as well as philosophers, semioticians, art historians, musicians, and musicologists) in an attempt to account for "the analysis of the Postmodern episteme."[2] Feyerabend, Shapiro, Glass, Eco, alongside Frampton, Eisenman, Purini . . . Among these contributions, there is also that of Jacques Derrida. The issue includes the transcription of a conversation between the editors and Derrida, held on April 24, 1985, at Yale University.[3] This short text includes a few fragments in which the philosopher's voice is quoted, referred to, and inscribed. It is likely that the editors realized too late during the conversation that they addressed the wrong person. However, they were not the only ones to consider Derrida the father of postmodern culture (an idea that is still alive today). This may explain the short transcription: despite the resistances of the text, it is evident that Derrida distances himself from the topic (the fragment) as well as from the frame (the analysis of a so called postmodern episteme):

> I am not happy with the concept of collage. I never use it as such. It is a traditional concept. Collage implies fragment, and that implies that there is a proper body the fragment belongs to. It is a kind

97

of disintegration and at the same time the memory of an integral body. The forms I am interested in—the forms of my desire—are not of that sort . . . a lot of people think of deconstruction as close to this disintegration. That is not the meaning of deconstruction.[4]

Derrida's contribution would have been out of context. But what are the limits of the context? What identifies the text by demarcating it from other texts, and what would be outside of the context? These are the questions Derrida's writing takes up in order to reinscribe them into the space of our writing, of the general writing that inscribes us and makes us inscribe. "*There is nothing outside the text* [Il n'y a pas de hors-texte],"[5] he would have noted. Let us read the fragment of Derrida's voice that concludes the editors' intervention:

> I must confess, I have no model. If there is one, I have the feeling my architectural model must be read in my text. So *Glas* or *La carte Postale* [*The Postcard*] is . . . an organization of space. *Glas* for instance is not only a book on the theme of the column in Hegel. It is in itself an architecture, an architectural artifact. That is my only answer, a very modest one. I have the feeling that my repressed desire for music and architecture comes back through my writing and what interests me in writing, beside the content or the thesis, is the form, the spatial form . . .
> I am unable to draw out of my text an architectural model. But if there is one, well read the text. Inhabit the text if you can.[6]

This is already more than a fragment. Three fragments. We do not know why the editors of the issue included it as a succession of three fragments and not as a unique piece. Nor we can find a reason from the context. Are these extrapolations from a larger discourse? Is there anything missing between these fragments? What? Why are they cut? On the other hand, beyond the quotation marks that open and close the three fragments, nothing guarantees that they must be attributed to Derrida. The account is not even countersigned by the philosopher but only by the curators. Let us take for granted this attribution and thus the paternity of the quoted text and the transparency of the transcription of Derrida's speech, even if we do not know if he spoke in French or in English (Who/what guarantees the paternity of the text? Of this text as of any other? Of the text as a work, an architectural work, for instance. A signature? Is the signature a text? Inside or outside the signed text? Does it belong to the text of which it marks the belonging?). Without knowing, we have already taken place in the space where we are inscribed, we are texts inhabited, more or less clandestinely, by urging questions related to the status of the text, of signature and work . . . We are texts where, precisely for these reasons, the spatial organization of writing plays an important role, although not a decisive one. We may even consider them architectural artifacts (and not works). *Glas* would thus be an architectural artifact. How should we listen to this voice? It may sound like Derrida's attempt to escape the question of architecture and protect himself behind a declaration of incompetence, or like one of Derrida's *coups-de-théâtre*. Certainly, this is a provocation: "Inhabit the text if you can."

I will try to address this question: *Glas* is certainly Derrida's most enigmatic work, and it is the least quoted, even among the philosopher's most faithful interpreters. It is an early provocation that is not immune from pretention, a testimony of the avant-garde spirit of turbulent years (1974), but this has already been said. Let us have a look at the book, even if it is not easy to describe it. It has the shape of an *album*: it is wider than it is tall, and it breaks with the classical proportions of a book by increasing the surface, the extension of the plane. It is a parallelepiped where horizontality prevails over verticality. The page is divided into two columns of writing: on the left side, we have Hegel, the philosopher of absolute knowledge and, on the right side, Jean Genet, the outlaw poet. The page is without notes and exact bibliographical references. The body of writing on the two columns is of different shapes and varies according to the extension of the text. In each column, the apparently main argument develops through portions of text that are more or less extended (from a few lines to several pages) and separated by more or less extended intervals. Furthermore, we encounter more or less extended insertions of other texts of various kinds, within a single portion. These insertions are taken from Hegel's correspondence with his wife, sister, friends, and colleagues; from Kant, Marx, Feuerbach, Freud, Saussure, Sartre, Lacan, Fonagy, as well as from etymological dictionaries, botanical treatises . . . Some insertions are also inscribed within the body of the main columns, on their sides, sometimes they come to double a column into two. Finally, the text is without conclusion. In the right column, it ends as follows: "What I had dreaded (*redouté*), naturally, already, republishes itself (*se réédite*). Today, here, now, the debris of (*le débris de*)"[7] An "open," "unfinished" work, we may say, in the style of the avant-garde. However, the text is not merely open, as it alludes to a continuation along the line of time, to an accomplishment of the work beyond the text. In the end, *Glas* returns where it has begun without losing the circle.[8] Here, the open and the unfinished have to do with the spatial dimension that produces the text (in an objective as well as subjective meaning), with the volume of the text rather than with the line of its apparent development (especially, in the grafting and interweaving together of lines and volumes). At first sight, therefore, the structure of the text seems to be quite fragmentary and baroque, if not chaotic and confused, without head or tail: an arrogant challenge in search of a meaning, able to discourage even the most optimistic interpreter. Before *Glas* we may stop and say: it is a formal exercise in the style of the literary French avant-garde that follows the example of Mallarmé's *blancs*, of Lettrist and Dadaist experiments, a sort of philosophical ready-made, a meaningless one, from the perspective of the so-called content. Responding to the invitation and, perhaps, the challenge of the master of the house, let us try to enter and "inhabit the text." The habitual (obsessive, unbearable?) reading of Derrida's text prevents us from rejecting the invitation too quickly. First, if *Glas* challenges the conventional norms of the composition of a book, this is for a precise reason that had already been formulated in *Of Grammatology*, the matrix-text of Derrida's writing:

> The good writing has therefore always been comprehended. Comprehended as that which had to be comprehended: within a nature or a natural law, created or not, but first thought within an eternal presence. Comprehended, therefore, within a totality, and enveloped in a volume or a book. The idea of the book is the idea of a totality, finite or infinite, of the signifier; this totality of the signifier cannot be a totality, unless a totality constituted by the signified preexists it, supervises its inscriptions and its signs, and is independent of it in its ideality. The idea of the book, which always refers to a natural totality, is profoundly alien to the sense of writing. It is the encyclopedic protection of theology and of logocentrism against the disruption of writing, against its aphoristic energy, and, as I shall specify later, against difference in general. If I distinguish the text from the book, I shall say that the destruction of the book, as it is now under way in all domains, denudes the surface of the text. That necessary violence responds to a violence that was no less necessary.[9]

The idea of book is structurally solidary with the system of the metaphysics of presence that imposes itself under the heading of *Logos*. A system—that of Western culture, from Plato to Saussure—that is grounded on the privilege of speech understood as a natural, spontaneous, immediate, and accomplished expression of ideality, that is, as a meaning that is supposed to be constituted by itself and fully present in the intimacy of a consciousness (soul, subject, etc.), which, in turn, is supposed to be present to itself in the production and expression of its own meanings. In this system, writing has always been thought as a merely empirical instrument at the service of speech and thus as a system of conventional representation designated for the transmission of a meaning whose production is independent. It is on this privilege of speech, the very element of logos, that the history of phonetico-alphabetic writing has been taking on the shape of our history, that is, its myth, given that a purely phonetic writing is impossible by fact as well as by right. This holds not only because phonetic writing cannot work without a set of diacritical signs deprived of phonic correspondence but, more radically, because it needs spacing, which, before any distinction between the phonic and the graphic, grants the differential variation of the constitutive elements of the sign and thus the production of effects of sense (and not of autonomous and independent meanings). As is well known, Derrida draws the inescapable consequences of Saussure's lesson to turn them against Saussure himself (against the phonological privilege that still binds the Swiss linguist to metaphysics):

> Saussure first of all is the thinker who put *the arbitrary character of the sign* and the *differential character* of the sign at the very foundation of general semiology, particularly linguistic. And, as we know, these two motifs—arbitrary and differential—are inseparable in his view. There can be arbitrariness only because the system is constituted solely by the differences in terms, and not by their plenitude. The elements of significations function due not to the compact force of their nuclei but rather to the network of the oppositions that distinguishes them, and then relates them one to another. "arbitrary" and "differential," says Saussure, "are two correlative characteristics." Now, this principle of difference, as the condition

for signification, affects the *totality* of the sign, that is the sign as both signified and signifier. . . . The first consequence to be drawn from this is that the signified concept is never present in and of itself, in a sufficient presence that would refer only to itself. Essentially and lawfully, every concept is inscribed in a chain or in a system within which it refers to the other, to other concepts, by means of the systematic play of differences.[10]

Now, spacing makes signification possible by breaking the compact unity of the sign, in particular, of speech, traditionally understood as the expression of a unique meaning that is autonomous in itself, independent of the signifier, and designated through its more or less transparent expression. Furthermore, at a greater level of complexity and extension of the signifying chain, spacing makes every kind of intervention possible: extrapolations, reinscription, quotations (but also cuts, concealments, lapses, removals, etc.) and thus the production and acknowledgment of effects of sense that are different and relatively independent from the sovereign signification that the signifying chain must slavishly represent. These effects of sense are finally independent of the presence of consciousness that must find its full accomplishment in the signifying chain. Spacing thus makes the production of these effects possible as it exposes this production to the absolute and infinite loss of absolute and infinite sense. One cannot be without the other. This is what writing shows once it is emancipated from *logocentric* repression, from the oppression of presence. In order to see how this writing comes out, it is thus necessary to deconstruct the idea of the book and, in particular, to dissociate the book from what binds it to *logocentrism*, the metaphysics of presence, the myth of the phonetico-alphabetic writing, the linear model:

The linear norm was never able to impose itself absolutely for the very reasons that intrinsically circumscribed graphic phoneticism. We now know them; these limits came into being at the same time as the possibility of what they limited, they opened what they finished and we have already named them: discreteness, différance, spacing. The production of the linear norm thus emphasized these limits and marked the concepts of symbol and language. The process of linearization, as Leroi-Gourhan describes it on a very vast historical scale, and the Jakobsonian critique of Saussure's linearist concept, must be thought of together. The "line" represents only a particular model, whatever might be its privilege. This model has become a model and, as a model, it remains inaccessible. If one allows that the linearity of language entails this vulgar and mundane concept of temporality (homogeneous, dominated by the form of the now and the ideal of continuous movement, straight or circular) which Heidegger shows to be the intrinsic determining concept of all ontology from Aristotle to Hegel, the meditation upon writing and the deconstruction of the history of philosophy become inseparable.[11]

This page contains the whole program of deconstruction, and it would require an infinite commentary. I limit myself to remarking that, through a dense network of references to Leroi-Gourhan, Derrida affirms that the model of linear writing has imposed itself historically through "the repression of pluri-dimensional symbolic thought."[12] This is what has been removed and what we must desediment through the deconstruction of the Book:

> The end of linear writing is indeed the end of the book, even if, even today, it is within the form of a book that new writings—literary or theoretical—allow themselves to be, for better or for worse, encased.

It is less a question of confiding new writings to the envelope of a book than of finally reading what wrote itself between the lines in the volumes. That is why, beginning to write without the line, one begins also to reread past writing according to a different organization of space. If today the problem of reading occupies the forefront of science, it is because of this suspense between two ages of writing. Because we are beginning to write, to write differently, we must reread differently.[13]

Therefore, *Glas* stands out on the horizon. We know enough to understand that it is much more (or less) than an early provocation; the stakes are higher, perhaps the highest possible (or they are the lowest ones, what remains of all stakes). We must write according to another spatial organization, a no longer linear but multidimensional organization, in which spacing is not submitted to the line or circle of the metaphysical temporality that underlies and produces the Idea and the closed form of the Book but is able to disclose the space where the traces of a text are inscribed, sedimented, and articulated. The trace must be the finite and material element of a composition that takes on the shape of an architectural product. Simultaneously, we must start rereading the texts of the past as architectural artifacts, we must again get used to recognizing under the remains of the Ideal of the Book certain architectures constructed according to certain purposes and functions and thus at the order of the metaphysics of presence: an ideal, full, intact, pure, infinite, eternal, and absolute presence, where there are no traces of the difference and spacing that have made its erection possible.

So, let us begin again to read *Glas* and the books that are inscribed in it (Will we finish at some point? We will not, hopefully, but yes, we will, necessarily. Meanwhile, we keep on writing). Let us rewrite according to another spatial organization. In particular, displacing the linearity of writing, we attempt to detect the dense weave of articulations and relations that make up the text and prevent it from closing upon itself, but not from producing effects of sense. Let's try to enter this house, which is still strange and yet a little more familiar. Despite the disorder, let me follow the rules of the host:

> First two columns. Truncated top and bottom, and also carved in their sides: incisions, tattoos, incrustations. A first reading can proceed as though two texts set up the one against the other or the one without the other did not communicate with each other. And in a certain deliberate way that remains true, as to pretext, object, language, style, rhythm, law. A *dialectic* on the one side, a *galactic* on the other, heterogeneous and yet indiscernible in their effects, at times to the point of hallucination. Between them the clapper of another text, one might say of another "logic"... For anyone attached to the signature, the corpus and the proper, let us declare that by putting into play, or rather into pieces, my name, my body and my seal, I by the same token elaborate those of the one named Hegel in his column, and those of the one named Genet in the other. It will be seen why—chance and necessity—those two. So the thing rises, details and detaches itself in two turns, and the incessant acceleration of a turn-by-turn. In their infinite solitude, the two colossi exchange countless overlaps, winks, double each other up at every opportunity, penetrate each other, stick and unstick, passing into each other, between one and into the other. Each column here figures a *colossus*, the name given to the dead man's double, to the substitute of his erection. More than one, before all.[14]

Above all, I must remark that I am quoting from the text entitled "Prière d'inserer," a folded sheet, of a size that is different from that of the page of *Glas*, where it is inserted, free from the rest. It is inside and outside the text. A text that is different from the text in which it is inscribed and *which* it seems to introduce. The space of reading seems to have been already affected by this insertion. Second, we must read two columns of writing as architectural artifacts: two columns that are erected and stand out on account of a supposed autonomy: the autonomy of the work, of the Book, granted by the signature of the author (subject, consciousness, etc.). In this case, Hegel's work, on one side, and Genet's work, on the other side. Two works that, at first glance, do not seem to communicate in any way: on the one hand, the elevation of finite consciousness to Absolute Spirit, through the sublimation of the difference of sexual desire within the wedding and family, the irreducible condition of the State. On the other hand, the apotheosis of the outlaw who passes through the inversion of any bourgeois rule— above all, the rule that sustains sexual difference—through the exaltation of any possible sordidness, which it finds in the celebration of its glory. Certainly, if they had encountered one another, Hegel and Genet would not have spoken (unless . . .)

However, as in Christian churches where columns of varying orders, taken from different places and times, sustain another building, *Glas* sets up their frame and builds another text, another architectural artifact, according to another spatial organization that allows us to acknowledge and read at once the two columns as composing elements of the same architecture. *Glas* consists in this frame that exposes what makes it possible: between the two columns, the clapper [*battant*] of another text, of another logic: spacing:

> Let us space (*espaçons*). The art of this text is the air it causes to circulate between its screens (*entre ses paravents*). The chainings are invisible, everything seems improvised or juxtaposed. This text induces by agglutinating rather than demonstrating, by coupling and decoupling, gluing and ungluing (*en accolant et en décollant*) rather than

by exhibiting the continuous, and analogical, instructive, suffocating necessity of a discursive rhetoric.[15]

In the frame of *Glas*, Hegel's and Genet's works are opposed like two columns, two towers that are one in front of the other, thus erected according to the same logic. According to the logic of opposition, that of the metaphysics of presence—our logic—the opposite cannot but reproduce the logic that it is opposed to, if only by inverting it. Genet's inversion is anything but "*antierection*: the time of erection countered (*contrée*), overlapped (*découpée*) to its contrary."[16] In particular, Genet, as well as Hegel, believes in the power of *Logos*, the idealizing and sublimating power of the act of naming, through which the named thing is absolved of its finite contingency and lifted to the element of ideality as infinite, absolute, and pure. Through this act, the human being (Adam), by means of Logos, is sublimated into the divine. Certainly, we should go into *Glas*, take the time required to explore its corners more than once, in order to sustain and justify this reading. I will limit myself to highlighting some traces. Above all, let me requote a passage from Genet, inscribed in *Glas*:

> These papers are their graves (*tombeau*). But I shall transmit their name far down the ages. This name alone will remain in the future, divested of its object. . . . If I take leave of this book, I take leave of what can be related. The remain(s) is ineffable (*le reste est indicible*). I say no more and walk barefoot.[17]

However, the divine filiation with which the *genêt* is affected is an immaculate conception, permit the son to take—therefore to leave—all the places, to sleep all alone, here with the father in (it)self, there with actual mother (ansich*seinede Vater und nur eine* wirkliche *Mutter*, but *nur eine* is the best) as in *absolute religion*, that is, on the (representative) threshold of absolute knowledge where the *glas* finally returns (close) by self, resounds, reflects itself for (it) self, admires its glory and is equal to itself.[18]

Therefore, Genet's work, once inscribed within the frame of *Glas*, can no longer be entirely solved, absolved, detached from the act of absolute self-naming to which it aims. To realize/idealize itself as such, it cannot but go through the erection of a column of writing, and thus it must leave the traces of its finite and contingent passage. It must constitute a funerary monument that guards the rest of what passed away and thus doubles the passage itself by displaying its irreducible and structural undecidability: "*Glas* is written neither one way nor the other [*ni d'un côté, ni de l'autre*], the one counting on the other to relieve the double's failure [*défaillance*], the colossus the column, the column the colossus. *Glas* strikes between the two."[19] The logic of the metaphysics of presence, as well as that of the Book, is grounded and sustained by the removal of spacing that makes possible at the same time as impossible its realization: "The structure of the tower is such that its construction returns, stone by stone, to its destruction: one tower, two towers, one is (without) the other."[20] Once we recognize the work (that of Hegel, as well as Genet's, or ours . . .) as an architectural artifact and thus as a frame of differentiated elements, its erection necessarily implies the possibility of its deconstruction. On the one hand, we have the impossibility of the accomplished realization, the impossibility of solving the spacing of the elements that materially make it up—traces and text—into a full totality that would be autonomous and independent from those elements that it aims to master. On the other hand, it implies the possibility of dissociating and rearticulating, reinscribing the elements that materially compose it, independently of the explicit intentions of the author (the sovereign presence of consciousness, of *logos*) of which the work would be the accomplished manifestation. Spacing entails the possibility of detecting complex relations—intersections, analogies, juxtapositions, inversions—between the constitutive elements and structures of works that are supposed to be accomplished totalities, closed upon themselves, and strangers to one another. Therefore, the ability to elaborate, out of these differentiated elements, architectural artifacts that can produce effects of sense that are not predicted by the Idea of the Book, effects of sense that exhibit the *défaillance* of the sovereignty of the *logos* as the condition of the production of sense, understood as spacing, spatial organization, production of traces and texts: "This is why there are only traces here, traces of traces without tracing, or, if you wish, tracings that only track and retrace other texts."[21] I can't go any further for now. We have just trespassed the border, drafted the general plan of arche-writing at work in *Glas*, detected a few passages. The topography and volumetry of *Glas* are still to be traced, starting from the detailed analysis of the effects of articulation between the graphic composition, the spacing of the text, and thematic contents. In particular, where we have the passage from the phallic column to the statue, through the colossus called Memnon, the pyramid, the labyrinth, the Sphinx, etc., which is, for Hegel, the beginning of architecture. Where erection *tombe*—in French: a funeral monument and the third person of the verb "falling"—prison, scaffolds, catafalques, crypts, bathrooms, and cylinders are at play:

> Now this book *presents itself* as a volume *of* cylindric columns, writes *on* pierced, incrusted, breached, tattooed cylindric columns, on them then, but also *around* them, *against* them, *between* them that are, through and through, tongue and text. *Kulindros* always names a round body, a pyramid, or obelisks, of other columns . . . *Kulindros* is also occasionally a rolled manuscript, a parchment scroll. So one is never enclosed in the column of one single tongue.[22]

NOTES

Introduction

1. Interview with Eva Mayer in 1984. Published in V. M. Lampugnani (ed.), *Der Abenteuer den Ideen: Architektur und Philosophie seit industriellen Revolution* (Berlin: Staatliche Museen, National Galerie, 1984).
2. Conversation with Peter Eisenman, published in the magazine *Any 0* (March–May 1993).
3. Derrida presents the special issue of "Cahier du CCI" devoted to this collaboration: *Mesure par mesure: Architecture et Philosophie* (Paris: Centre George Pompidou, 1987). Cf. J. Derrida, "Fifty-Two Aphorisms for a Foreword," in J. Derrida, *Psyche: Inventions of the Other, Volume II*, ed. P. Kamuf and E. Rottenberg (Stanford: Stanford University Press, 2008).
4. J. Derrida, "No (Point of) Madness—Maintaining Architecture," in J. Derrida, *Psyche: Inventions of the Other, Volume II*. First published as "Point de folies—Maintenant l'architecture," in B. Tschumi, *La case vide: La Villette* (London: Architectural Association, 1986).
5. Cf. J. Kipnis and T. Leeser (eds.), *Chora L Works: Jacques Derrida and Peter Eisenman* (New York: Monacelli Press, 1997).
6. Cf. J. Derrida, B. Tschumi, M. Wigley, "Invitation to Discussion," *Columbia Documents of Architecture and Theory* 1 (1992): 7–22.
7. Cf. J. Derrida, K. Foster, and W. Wenders, "The Berlin City Forum," *Architectural Design* 26.11/12 (1992): 46–53.

8. Cf. J. Derrida, "Générations d'une ville: mémoire, prophétie, responsabilité," in Alena Novotná Galard and Petr Kratochvíl (eds.), *Prague: Avenir d'une ville historique capitale* (Paris: l'Aube, 1992), 39–53.

9. Cf. J. Derrida, "On between the Lines," in D. Libeskind, *Radix-Matrix* (Munich/New York: Prestel, 1997), 110–115.

10. Cf. J. Derrida, "Summary of Impromptu Remarks," in C. C. Davidson and J. Kipnis (eds.), *Anyone* (New York: Rizzoli, 1991), and J. Derrida, "Faxtexture," in C. C. Davidson (ed.), *Anywhere* (New York: Rizzoli, 1992).

11. The term "deconstructivism" was invented by P. Johnson and M. Wigley, the editors of the exhibition catalogue *Deconstructivist Architecture*; it referred to a movement including the autonomous and original work of various architects. See P. Johnson and M. Wigley (eds.), *Deconstructivist Architecture* (New York: The Museum of Modern Art, 1988). According to Johnson and Wigley (ibid., 11), architectural deconstructivism has nothing to do with philosophical deconstructivism and is rather a movement within the architectural tradition, attached to "Russian constructivism," even if from a critical perspective. However, it is worth recalling that they write in 1988 and thus right after the failed collaboration between Derrida and Eisenman for La Villette park in Paris and the subsequent controversy. I will address this moment in the chapter entitled "Divergent Traces."

12. Derrida, "No (Point of) Madness—Maintaining Architecture," 88.

13. For an introduction to Derrida's work and an interpretation of deconstruction, its procedures, and targets, see R. Gasché, *The Tain of the Mirror: Derrida and the Philosophy of Reflection* (Cambridge/London: Harvard University Press, 1986), and G. Bennington, "Derridabase," in G. Bennington and J. Derrida, *Derrida*, trans. G. Bennington (Chicago: University of Chicago Press, 1993).

14. "No (Point of) Madness—Maintaining Architecture," 92.

15. Cf. Derrida, "Fifty-Two Aphorisms for a Foreword," 125.

16. Ibid., 120.

17. On Plato, cf. J. Derrida, "Plato's Pharmacy," in *Dissémination*, trans. B. Johnson (London: Athlone Press, 1981). The examination of Freud's uncanny can be found throughout Derrida's work and in particular in *Specters of Marx: The State of the Debt, the Work of Mourning and the New International*, trans. P. Kamuf (New York/London: Routledge, 1994). It is worth recalling that the term often recurs in the interventions on architecture, and the French *hanter* (haunting) means "tormenting," "being obsessed" in a pathological sense, but it also refers to the presence of ghosts: a haunted house (*une maison hantée*) means a "house visited by ghosts." On the uncanny in architecture, see the excellent analyses in A. Vidler, *The Architectural Uncanny: Essays in the Modern Unhomely* (Cambridge/London: MIT Press, 1992). Regarding the architectonic dimension of Derrida's work before the encounter with Tschumi and Eisenman, see M. Wigley, *The Architecture of Deconstruction: Derrida's Haunt* (Cambridge/London: MIT Press, 1993). Although this text had the merit of highlighting the interest of deconstruction in architecture and, more generally, in the question of space, it betrays serious limits. In particular, Wigley, who is a theorist of architecture, does not understand the philosophical dimension of the main deconstructive notions elaborated by Derrida, such as "différance," "arche-writing," or "arche-trace," and "spacing." More generally, he overlooks the fundamentally temporal dimension of the metaphysics of presence, the fact that the metaphysical determination of presence depends on the determination of temporality on the basis of the present understood as a punctual instant, which is indivisible and detached from the becoming, of which it would be the elementary and irreducible condition. The deconstruction of the metaphysics of presence requires the deconstruction of this conception of temporality, first and necessarily. It is from this perspective that Derrida introduces the notion of spacing, which does not mean, as Wigley suggests, "the 'becoming space' of space" (74, between brackets Wigley quotes from Derrida's *Of Grammatology*) but "the becoming-space of time and the becoming-time of space," thus referring to "the

articulation of space and time" (*Of Grammatology*, 68). It is from this rearticulation of space and time that Derrida deconstructs their metaphysical opposition. In Wigley's book, there are no traces of the problem of temporality and of spatiotemporal articulation (also the word "time" is missing). And this is why Wigley can reduce deconstruction to a sort of rehabilitation of spatiality within the philosophical tradition. On the other hand, given the distortion of the aforementioned passage from *Of Grammatology*, we may suspect that this reduction is intentional and conscious: an illegitimate stretch. As we will see, Derrida elaborates the notion of arche-writing precisely in view of the deconstruction of the classical opposition of space and time. By arche-writing, he describes the conditions of possibility of the construction of meaning in general for a consciousness in general. Briefly, the presence of the meaning (that is supposedly internal to consciousness) is an effect of the trace (that should be external) inscribed in a structurally open system of referrals, and not, as we would say commonly, its cause. Hence, all forms of the inscription of the meaning in a trace constitute different possibilities conditioned by arche-writing. So-called writing is just one of these possibilities and not the only one, as Wigley argues (80–81), the one privileged by Derrida in order to designate architectural writing or architecture as writing. In fact, Derrida takes architecture as an example of a "multidimensional" writing, able to demystify the privilege of the linear alphabetic writing that characterizes the tradition of the metaphysics of presence. Wigley misunderstands this point as he does not demarcate arche-writing from empirical writing and thus cannot grasp the limitless generalization that the notion of "text" undergoes from within the perspective opened up by Derrida through arche-writing. Finally, the critical hypothesis that ends Wigley's book misses its target: "And if deconstruction is spacing in this sense, what about deconstructive discourse? If there is no discourse that is not a space and no space without spacing, what would be the space of a discourse about spacing? Is it even possible to have such a discourse? After all, spacing is precisely that which withdraws from discourse and opens it to something other. This opening can therefore never simply be the object of a discourse" (197). What I have just said should prove that Wigley's hypothesis is unjustified. Let me add that, by virtue of the notion of arche-writing and of the derived conception of the general text, a text (even a discourse, strictly speaking) has already been opened onto alterity in general, since this opening constitutes its irreducible condition of possibility: the possibility of the referral that structures the trace as such. Later, I will make these affirmations explicit. To some extent, one may read the present volume as a critical response to Wigley's book, even if the latter is not mentioned, and in particular to the question raised at the end of *The Architecture of Deconstruction: Derrida's Haunt*: "Architecture remains the Achilles heel of deconstructive discourse. The strength of that discourse depends on the veiling of its systemic weakness for architecture, a traditional weakness that structures the discourse as such and needs to be interrogated, especially when the question of deconstruction and architecture is being explicitly raised. Not only has such an interrogation hardly even begun here, but this text must immediately be subjected to it" (219).

18. Derrida, "No (Point of) Madness—Maintaining Architecture," 92.

19. Ibid.

20. See J. Derrida, "Some Statements and Truisms about Neologism, Newisms, Postisms, Parasitisms and Other Small Seismisms," in D. Carrol (ed.), *The State of "Theory": History, Art and Critical Discourse* (New York: Columbia University Press, 1990).

21. "No (Point of) Madness—Maintaining Architecture," 91.

22. Ibid., 88.

Chapter 1. The Law of the Oikos

1. Derrida, "No (Point of) Madness—Maintaining Architecture," 92.

2. Ibid.

3. Ibid., 90.
4. Ibid., 91.
5. Ibid., 92.
6. J. Derrida, "Khōra," in J. Derrida, *On the Name*, trans. I. McLeod (Stanford: Stanford University Press, 1995). It was first published in Kipnis and T. Leeser, *Chora L Works*. For a reading of "Khōra" from the architectural point of view, see A. Vidler, "Nothing to Do with Architecture," *Gray Room* 21 (2005): 112–127.
7. Cf. M. Heidegger, *Introduction to Metaphysics*, trans. G. Fried and R. Polt (New Haven/London: Yale University Press, 2000), 69.
8. Derrida, "No (Point of) Madness—Maintaining Architecture," 91.
9. Derrida, "Plato's Pharmacy," 103.
10. Ibid., 103–133.
11. J. Derrida, "Nationalité et nationalisme philosophique: Mythos, logos, topos," 1985/1986, unpublished seminar (Caen: Archive Derrida, IMEC).
12. Plato, *Timaeus*, 17c.
13. Erichthonius, son of Hephaestus and Gaia, the earth. Hephaestus was promised to Athena, but the latter escaped the nuptial *thalamus*. Therefore, Hephaestus's seed missed the target and fell on the earth, fertilizing it. The tradition consecrated Erichthonius as the king of Athens, father of the Athenian *genos*, which for this reason considered itself the only Greek population that was authentically autochthonous. Protector of the Acropolis of Athens, and founder of the temple dedicated to Athena on the top of the Acropolis, Erichthonius was also considered the founder of the Pan-Athenians. The myth of autochthony played an ideological function in the fifth century BCE as a support of the Athenian identity and of the latter's superiority over the other Greek populations. This identity was supposed to be pure from any contamination, from the other as well as with the female element. Even if from opposite perspectives, Plato and Pericles will go back to this point in order to justify democracy as the

regime of Athens, by grounding political equality (*Isonomia*) on the equality derived from the heroic origin of ethnicity (*Eugenia*). Nicole Loraux, a disciple of Vernant but also close to Derrida, dedicated foundational works to the theme of Athenian autochthony as an identitary paradigm grounded on the exclusion of the other. In particular, see N. Loraux, *L'invention d'Athénes: Histoire de l'oraison funèbre dans la cité classique* (Paris/la Haye: Mouton/Éd. De l'EHESS, 1981); N. Loraux, *The Children of Athena: Athenian Ideas about Citizenship and the Division between the Sexes*, trans. C. Levine (Princeton: Princeton University Press, 1993); N. Loraux, *Né de la terre* (Paris: Seuil, 1996). It is important to notice that about the theme of the Athenians' autochthony, Derrida refers extensively to Loraux, *The Children of Athena*. This text will be a very important reference for *The Politics of Friendship*, where he undertakes the deconstruction of the link that binds democracy to autochthony, to the attachment to a political equality of ethnic-territorial nature.

14. On the politico-religious function of the Pan-Athenians, see A. Queyrel, *Athènes. La cité archaïque et classique* (Paris: Picard, 2003), 247–252. Queyrel highlights the importance of the architectural setting that must emphasize the sense of identity and belonging of the Athenians as well as impress the foreigners invited from everywhere in Greece to attend. It is precisely the representation on the Ionic frieze to offer a synthesis of the symbolic function of the Parthenon: cf. 251. The frieze includes 360 characters and "represents an uncommon subject for a religious building as it juxtaposes the frontons and metopes featuring gods and heroes with a relief staging mortals, the members of the heroic community of the city caught in the act of celebrating their divinity. The choice of representing the ceremony of the greatest feast in honor of the goddess celebrated by the monument glorifies the community of believers as well as the community itself."

15. Derrida, "Nationalité et nationalisme philosophique," session 1/22/1986.

16. Plato, *Timaeus*, 19b–c.

17. Derrida, "Khōra," 118.
18. Plato, *Timaeus*, 19e.
19. Derrida, "Khōra," 107.
20. Cf. Plato, *Timaeus*, 27d–28a.
21. Derrida, "Nationalité et nationalisme philosophique," session 1/22/1986.
22. Ibid.
23. Ibid. On the role played by Critias in the *Timaeus*, see J. Sallis, *Chorology: On Beginning in Plato's* Timaeus (Bloomington/Indianapolis: Indiana University Press, 1999), chap. "Remembrance of the City," 7–45.
24. Plato, *Timaeus*, 19a.
25. Derrida, "Khōra," 109.
26. From the perspective of architecture, we agree with the conclusions drawn by Vidler in the aforementioned article. However, once the law of the *oikos* is discovered, it is necessary to recognize that the "foundation of the polis" regulates both architecture and onto-cosmology. Cf. Vidler, "Nothing to Do with Architecture," 123: "The foundation of the polis, moreover, demands a replication of the cosmic constructs—the establishments of territories through geometry, their definition according to classes of inhabitants, and the careful exclusion of noncitizens of the polis into the worldly equivalent of chaos. In sum, the work of architecture."
27. Derrida, *Specters of Marx*, 102.
28. Ibid., 103.

Chapter 2. The House in Deconstruction

1. Cf. Derrida, "Khōra."
2. Derrida, "No (Point of) Madness—Maintaining Architecture," 90.
3. The list of four points, which Derrida himself designates as artificial, refers in a fashion that is evidently ironic to the

Geviert, the *squaring*, namely, to the Heideggerian *dwelling*, from which Derrida aims to demarcate himself.

4. Derrida, "No (Point of) Madness—Maintaining Architecture," 91.

5. J.-P. Vernant, *Mythe et Religion en Grèce ancienne*, in J.-P. Vernant, *œuvres*, vol. 1: *Religions, rationalités, politique* (Paris: Seuil, 2007), 847.

6. J. Rykwert, *The Dancing Column: On Order in Architecture* (Cambridge/London: MIT Press, 1999), 149.

7. Vernant, *Mythe et Religion en Grèce ancienne*, 848. Rykwert also highlights the intimate link between heroic cults and the foundation of Greek cities. He points out that the hero-founder could also be a mythic and legendary figure, as in the case of Athens. In particular, he remarks that the original position of the agora was linked to the funerary cult of the hero-founders: cf. J. Rykwert, *The Idea of a Town* (Cambridge: MIT Press, 1988 [1963]), 35: "Cities which were not known to have been founded by a 'historical hero' may well have devised one from fragments of myth. But historical persons who founded towns were, during their lifetime, given semi-heroic status and honoured as heroes after their death. It is not a case of arguing causally. The city had to be founded by a hero; only a hero could found a city. In the same way the Pindaric scholiast's assertion implies a polarity: the hero-founder had to be buried at the heart of the city; only the tomb of the hero-founder could guarantee that the city lived. Indeed, the assembly of the primitive *agora*, in the sense in which the word signifies the men and not the place, was often in the early literature attracted to a pre-existing tomb. The Greek *agora* continued to have connections with funerary cults as long as the *polis* remained a religious as well as a political force. The founder's commemoration that I have mentioned earlier, is the most striking instance of this side of civic religious life."

8. Cf. F. de Polignac, *Cults, Territory, and the Origins of the Greek City-State*, trans. J. Lloyd (Chicago: University of Chicago Press, 1995). The author of this excellent book argues that the

sanctuary (the ensemble constituted by temple, altar, and fence) is the very catalyzing element of the birth of the *polis*, from a symbolic as well as a concrete perspective. Indeed, he remarks, "the building of a monumental temple has sometimes been considered as a *Polis' birth certificate*" (20). The first urban concentration takes place around the sanctuary, which constitutes its center, whereas the peri-urban and extra-urban sanctuaries establish the borders of the territory by symbolizing the limit between the human and savage nature at the same time as by affirming the possession of soil for agriculture and farming, the property and thus the identity of the city against the identities of the other cities and, more generally, against foreigners. On the monumental sanctuary, cf. 87: "So the first thing that needs to be understood is the nature of the monumental sanctuary, for it was there that the *polis* took shape even as it gathered itself together around the cult and forged its own consciousness of an identity that both itself and others could recognize. There, in the sanctuary, the rites and the architecture, together with the representations of local myths and symbols, created a sacred space that was at once the heart and the frontier of the city, the organ of its constantly renewed constitution and the place of mediation in its relations—amicable or hostile—with the external world, both human and divine. This essential combination of qualities explains why it is that these sanctuaries were so famous: to know a city meant knowing the cult whose rites and images engendered the political society."

9. Herodotus, *The Histories*, trans. A. D. Godley (Cambridge: Harvard University Press, 1920), 8: 53–54: "The Persians took up a position on the hill opposite the acropolis, which the Athenians call the Areopagus, and besieged them in this way: they wrapped arrows in tar and set them on fire, and then shot them at the barricade. Still the besieged Athenians defended themselves, although they had come to the utmost danger and their barricade had failed them. When the Pisistratids proposed terms of surrender, they would not listen but contrived defenses such as rolling down boulders onto the barbarians when they came

near the gates. For a long time Xerxes was at a loss, unable to capture them. In time a way out of their difficulties was revealed to the barbarians, since according to the oracle all the mainland of Attica had to become subject to the Persians. In front of the acropolis, and behind the gates and the ascent, was a place where no one was on guard, since no one thought any man could go up that way. Here some men climbed up, near the sacred precinct of Cecrops' daughter Aglaurus, although the place was a sheer cliff. When the Athenians saw that they had ascended to the acropolis, some threw themselves off the wall and were killed, and others fled into the chamber. The Persians who had come up first turned to the gates, opened them, and murdered the suppliants. When they had levelled everything, they plundered the sacred precinct and set fire to the entire acropolis."

10. Thucydides, *The Peloponnesian War*, trans. R. Crawley (New York: Random House, 1951), 1: 89. "Meanwhile the Athenian people, after the departure of the barbarian from their country, at once proceeded to carry over their children and wives, and such property as they had left, from the places where they had deposited them, and prepared to rebuild their city and their walls. For only isolated portions of the circumference had been left standing, and most of the houses were in ruins; though a few remained, in which the Persian grandees had taken up their quarters."

11. Cf. R. Carpenter, *The Architects of the Parthenon* (Harmondsworth: Penguin Books, 1970).

12. J.-P. Vernant, *The Origins of Greek Thought* (Ithaca: Cornell University Press, 1982), 28: "The Mycenaean Manor, centered on the *megaron* [a great center hall] and the throne room, is a walled fortress, a chieftain's den, dominating and keeping watch over the plain at its feet. Constructed to withstand a siege, this citadel sheltered the quarters of the king's intimate associates, the military leaders and palace dignitaries, alongside the princely dwelling and its outbuildings. Its military role appears above all to have been defensive: it protected the royal treasury. Here, along with the reserves normally superintended, stocked, and

distributed by the palace in the region's economic plan, were gathered precious goods of a different sort, the products of a luxury trade: jewelry, cups, tripods, bowls, the work of goldsmiths, ornamented weapons, metal molds, rugs, embroidered fabrics. Symbols of power, instruments of personal prestige—in their opulence they were a fitting expression of royalty."

13. Ibid., 183. For the etymology of the word *polis* as derived from *acropolis*, fortress, we can trace it in a text by É. Benveniste, to whom Derrida has never stopped referring throughout his work. Cf. the entry "city and community" in É. Benveniste, *Le Vocabulaire des institutions indo-européennes. I. Économie, parenté, société* (Paris: Minuit, 1969), 281: "In Greek, *polis* still indicates in a historical age the sense of 'fortress, citadel' as Thucydides points out: 'The *acropolis* (citadel) is still called today *polis* by the Athenians' (II 15). This was the prehistorical meaning of the word, according to its correspondent ved. *Pūr* e lit. *pilìs* 'fortress.'"

Chapter 3. Jacques Derrida and the Politics of Architecture

1. Derrida, "No (Point of) Madness—Maintaining Architecture," 92.
2. Derrida, *Specters of Marx*, 82.
3. Derrida, "Plato's Pharmacy," 133.
4. Ibid., 133.
5. J. Derrida, *Specters of Marx*, 83. It is worth recalling that in Greek civilization the onto-political axiomatic is thoroughly formulated in Aristotle's *Politics*. See *The Complete Works of Aristotle*, ed. J. Barnes (Princeton: Princeton University Press, vol. 2, 1991): *Politics*, II 1, 1260b–1261a: "We will begin with the natural beginning of the subject. Three alternatives are conceivable: The members of a state must either have (1) all things or (2) nothing in common, or (3) some things in common and some not. That they should have nothing in common is clearly impossible, for the constitution is a community, and must at

any rate have a common place—one city will be in one place, and the citizens are those who share in that one city." Cf. also III 9, 1280b: "It is clear then that a state is not a mere society, having a common place, established for the prevention of mutual crime and for the sake of exchange. These are conditions without which a state cannot exist; but all of them together do not constitute a state, which is a community of families and aggregations of families in well-being, for the sake of a perfect and self-sufficing life. Such a community can only be established among those who live in the same place and intermarry."

6. In particular, on several occasions Derrida refers to the development of tele-technologies (from television to individual video camera, from mobile video telephone to internet), which plays a decisive role today in the deterritorialization of political, economic, commercial, and cultural relations and contributes to the constitution of a public space that is no longer attached to traditional territory availability. Cf. J. Derrida, "Faith and Knowledge: The Two Sources of 'Religion' at the Limits of Reason Alone," trans. S. Weber, in J. Derrida and G. Vattimo (eds.), *Religion* (Stanford: Stanford University Press, 1998). On this subject, see also: M. Naas, *Miracle and Machine: Jacques Derrida and the Two Sources of Religion, Science, and the Media* (New York: Fordham University Press, 2012). See also J. Derrida, "The Word Processor," in J. Derrida, *Paper Machine*, trans. R. Bowlby (Stanford: Stanford University Press, 2005).

7. Derrida, *Specters of Marx*, 83.

8. On democracy, see J. Derrida, *The Other Heading: Reflections on Today's Europe*, trans. P.-A. Brault and M. Naas (Bloomington: Indiana University Press, 1992); J. Derrida, *Rogues: Two Essays on Reason*, trans. P.-A. Brault and M. Naas (Stanford: Stanford University Press, 2005). See also M.-L. Mallet (ed.), *La Démocratie à venir: Autour de Jacques Derrida* (Paris: Galilée, 2004).

9. On this subject, see the seminal essay by J.-P. Vernant, "Hestia-Ermès: The Religious Expression of Space and Movement in Ancient Greece," in J.-P. Vernant, *Myth and Thought among the Greeks* (New York: Zone Books, 2006), 157–195. In particular,

Vernant recalls that, in the historical age we are interested in, the word *oikos* "has both a family and a territorial meaning." See also how the house must be for Socrates: Xenophon, *Memorabilia*, trans. A. L. Bonnette (Ithaca: Cornell University Press, 1994): III, 8, 4–10: "In one word, there where in all seasons one can find shelter in the most pleasant way and one's goods can be kept in the utmost safety, this place would rightly be the sweetest and coziest house."

10. Derrida, "No (Point of) Madness—Maintaining Architecture," 92.

11. Ibid.

12. Ibid.

13. Ibid., 88.

14. Derrida, "Fifty-Two Aphorisms for a Foreword," 126.

15. J. Derrida, P. Brunette, D. Wills, "The Spatial Arts: An Interview with Jacques Derrida," in P. Brunette and D. Wills (eds.), *Deconstruction and the Visual Arts: Art, Media, Architecture* (Cambridge: Cambridge University Press, 1994), 26.

16. Ibid.

17. Ibid., 27.

18. J. Derrida, *The Politics of Friendship*, trans. G. Collins (London/New York: Verso, 2005), 219.

19. Ibid., 250.

20. On hospitality, see J. Derrida and A. Dufourmantelle, *Of Hospitality*, trans. R. Bowlby (Stanford: Stanford University Press, 2000); J. Derrida, "Hospitality," *Angelaki: Journal of the Theoretical Humanities* 5.3 (December 2000): 13–18; J. Derrida, "Hospitality," in J. Derrida, *Acts of Religion*, ed. G. Anidjar (New York/London: Routledge, 2002).

21. Derrida, Forster, and Wenders, "Berlin City Forum."

22. Derrida, "Générations d'une ville: mémoire, prophétie, responsabilité."

23. Ibid., 25.

24. F. Kafka, "The City Coat of Arms," in F. Kafka, *The Great Wall of China: Stories and Reflections* (New York: Schocken Books, 1946), 234.

25. Ibid.
26. J. Derrida, "Générations d'une ville: mémoire, prophétie, responsabilité," 34.
27. Ibid., 34.
28. Derrida, "Faxtexture," 126.

Chapter 4. Mythographies

1. Derrida, "No (Point of) Madness—Maintaining Architecture," 92.
2. Cf. R. Gasché, *Views and Interviews: On "Deconstruction" in America* (Aurora: The Davies Group, 2007), 17: "Are we already capable of the necessary attention to the law of composition and the rule of the play of his text? Are we sufficiently equipped to establish what—because of the strategies at work in his interpretations, the juxtaposition and confrontation of various positions, the complex relation between what his texts do and what they say, and so forth—is happening in them, and thus also prepared to read each one of them on the basis of the singular logic, law, or principle that organizes its performative, or rather, its event character?"
3. Derrida, "No (Point of) Madness—Maintaining Architecture," 88.
4. J. Derrida, *Of Grammatology*, trans. G. C. Spivak (Baltimore/ London: Johns Hopkins University Press, 1976), 86.
5. G. Vergani, P. Shinoda, and D. Kesler, "Fragments of a Conversation with Jacques Derrida," *Precis: The Journal of the Columbia University Graduate School of Architecture, Planning and Preservation, The Culture of Fragments* 6 (1987): 49.
6. J. Derrida and P. Eisenman, "Talking about Writing," *Any 0* (March–May 1993). To further strengthen our hypothesis, I refer to an unpublished text found at the Derrida Archives at the IMEC, in Caen. It is the transcription of the roundtable on *Deconstruction and Architecture* held in Madrid in 1996 (it is still unknown when it took place): J. Derrida, "Deconstruction

Philosophie, Deconstruction Architecture," unpublished seminar (Caen: IMEC Archives, Fond Derrida), DRR 192: "I would like to start with some general remarks on my relation to architecture. It should have never taken place. From the perspective of architects as well as from that of my work, there was a certain necessity of this encounter (. . .) I would like to say, as a premise, what, I believe, made necessary the appeal to architecture in deconstruction: above all, the elaboration of a deconstructive thought of the trace and writing took the shape of a thought of what I called *spacing* (*espacement*), that is, the interval, the opening of a space marked by intervals, by a between-two (*entre-deux*) and thus the becoming-space of time, a thought that cannot but encounter what is inscribed in space."

7. Derrida, *Of Grammatology*, 18.

8. Derrida, "No (Point of) Madness—Maintaining Architecture," 90.

9. J. Derrida, "The Pit and the Pyramid: Introduction to Hegel's Semiology," in J. Derrida, *Margins of Philosophy*, trans. A. Bass (Brighton: The Harvester Press, 1982), 82.

10. Sophocles, *Antigone*, 951–952 (trans. R. Gibbons and C. Segal [Oxford: Oxford University Press, 2003], 94). Quoted in J. Derrida, *Glas*, trans. J. P. Leavey Jr. and R. Rand (Lincoln/London: University of Nebraska Press, 1986), 145.

11. Plato, *Cratylus*, 400b–c. Quoted in Derrida, "The Pit and the Pyramid," 82.

12. Derrida, *Of Grammatology*, 70.

13. J. Derrida, *Edmund Husserl's Origin of Geometry. An Introduction*, trans. J. P. Leavey Jr. (Lincoln: University of Nebraska Press, 1989), 85.

14. Hence, the famous locution in *Of Grammatology*, 158: "There is nothing outside of the text [*Il n'y a pas de hors-texte*]" drops its arcane aura and is definitely distant from the hyper-hermeneutic declination that had prevailed for so long. If arche-writing is the irreducible condition of possibility of experience, then our experience is constituted as a weave of traces, it *is* a text, evidently not the text written and guarded in

libraries. Cf. J. Derrida, *Limited Inc.*, trans. S. Weber (Evanston: Northwestern University Press, 1988), 148: "I wanted to recall that the concept of text I propose is limited neither to the graphic, nor to the book, nor even to discourse, and even less to the semantic, representational, symbolic, ideal, or ideological sphere. What I call 'text' implies all the structures called 'real,' 'economic,' 'historical,' socio-institutional, in short: all possible referents. Another way of recalling once again that 'there is nothing outside the text.' That does not mean that all referents are suspended, denied, or enclosed in a book, as people have claimed, or have been naive enough to believe and to have accused me of believing. But it does mean that every referent, all reality has the structure of a differential trace, and that one cannot refer to this 'real' except in an interpretive experience. The latter neither yields meaning nor assumes it except in a movement of differential referring. *That's all.*"

15. Derrida, *Of Grammatology*, 74.

16. Ibid.

17. Ibid., 81.

18. In *Of Grammatology*, Derrida does not refer to a writing that is perhaps closer to him as well as to us, to phonetico-alphabetic writing and its tradition, a writing that perhaps inhabits our tradition: Jewish writing. This is not the place to open another abyss, but I invite the reader to compare a page from the Torah to a page from *Glas*.

19. Derrida, *Of Grammatology*, 85. Cf. A. Leroi-Gourhan, *Gesture and Speech*, trans. A. Bostock Berger (Cambridge/London: MIT Press, 1993). On "mythogram," see 191–210, in particular, 195: "Two languages, both springing from the same source, came into existence at the two poles of the operating field—the language of hearing, which is linked with the development of the sound-coordinating areas, and the language of sight, which in turn is connected with the development of the gesturecoordinating areas, the gestures being translated into graphic symbols. If this is so, it explains why the earliest known graphic signs are stark expressions of rhythmic values. Be that

as it may, graphic symbolism enjoys some independence from phonetic language because its content adds further dimensions to what phonetic language can only express in the dimension of time. The invention of writing, through the device of linearity, completely subordinated graphic to phonetic expression, but even today the relationship between language and graphic expression is one of coordination rather than subordination. An image possesses a dimensional freedom which writing must always lack. It can trigger the verbal process that culminates in the recital of a myth, but it is not attached to that process; its context disappears with the narrator. This explains the profuse spread of symbols in systems without linear writing. Many authors of works on primitive Chinese culture, Australian aborigines, North American Indians, or certain peoples of Black Africa speak of their mythological way of thinking in which the world order is integrated in an extraordinarily rich system of symbolic relationships. A number of these authors mention the very rich systems of graphic representation available to the peoples they observed. In each case, except perhaps that of the early Chinese where the records postdate the invention of writing, the groups of figures represented are coordinated in accordance with a system that is completely foreign to linear organization and consequently to any possibility of continuous phonetization. . . . Indeed in primitive societies mythology and multidimensional graphism usually coincide. If I had the courage to use words in their strict sense, I would be tempted to counterbalance 'mytho-logy'—a multidimensional construct based upon the verbal—with 'mytho-graphy,' its strict counterpart based upon the manual."

20. Derrida, *Of Grammatology*, 87.

21. Derrida, "No (Point of) Madness—Maintaining Architecture," 95.

Chapter 5. Writing Space

1. Derrida, *Of Grammatology*, 70.
2. Ibid., 86.

3. Ibid., 85. Cf. Leroi-Gourhan, *Gesture and Speech*, 191–210.
4. Derrida, "No (Point of) Madness—Maintaining Architecture," 88.
5. Cf. ibid., 87: "I am setting out on a road, or rather course, among other possible and concurrent ones."
6. Ibid., 95.
7. Ibid.
8. Ibid.
9. Ibid., 96.
10. B. Tschumi, *The Manhattan Transcripts* (London: Architectural Design, 1984).
11. Ibid., 6.
12. Cf. A. Vidler, "The Explosion of Space: Architecture and the Filmic Imaginary," *Assemblage* 21 (1993): 44–59. For Vidler, the intersection of architecture and cinema that characterizes Tschumi's earliest works is not so original within the architectural tradition. Rather, it is inscribed in the tradition of the historical avant-garde, of modernism itself, which looks at cinema as the modern art *par excellence* and, in particular, of Russian constructivism. Through an excellent reconstruction that goes back to Eisenstein (who writes *Editing and Architecture* in 1927), Vidler thus seems to confirm Wigley's thesis: architectural deconstructivism would be a movement that is essentially internal to the history of architecture. Cf. P. Johnson and M. Wigley, *Deconstructivist Architecture*, 11. However, if it is true that Tschumi makes an explicit reference to Kuleshov and Eisenstein's theories of editing, one must also acknowledge—with Derrida—that Tschumi's research is not only concerned with the intersection of cinema and architecture but also with other forms of the experience of space, especially the elaboration of notation systems able to record and reproduce the traces of the experience of space by detaching the latter from its supposedly aleatory contingency, at the same time as by deconstructing the traditional conventions of architectural presentation.
13. Tschumi, *The Manhattan Transcripts*, 8.
14. The passage mentioned by Tschumi without a bibliographical reference is from L. Wittgenstein, *Tractatus Logico-Philosophicus*,

trans. D. F. Pears and B. F. McGuinness (London/New York: Routledge, 2001), §5.6.

15. Tschumi, *The Manhattan Transcripts*, 9.

16. On the privilege of sight in architecture, cf. J. Pallasmaa, *The Eyes of the Skin: Architecture and the Senses* (Chichester: Wiley & Sons, 2005).

17. Tschumi, *The Manhattan Transcripts*, xxiii. Cf. L. Martin, "Transpositions: On the Intellectual Origins of Tschumi's Architectural Theory," *Assemblage* 11 (1990): 27, in which Tschumi's theoretical research is described as initially oriented to the elaboration of a different "experience of space" that draws together critically the different theoretical formulations inherited from tradition with regard to the space that is conceived, perceived, and experienced.

18. Tschumi, *The Manhattan Transcripts*, 7.

19. On the uncanny in architecture, cf. Vidler, *The Architectural Uncanny*, in particular, 113–117 are dedicated to *The Manhattan Transcripts* and La Villette park.

20. In cinematographic editing, the "jump-cut" indicates the cut of the central part of a sequence, a cut that retains the initial part and the final one, between which there is no temporal continuity. It is also called the "axis-cut." The object in movement seems to leap from one position to another. "Jump-cuts" are true leaps, cut frames, where one employs classical but not false connections, such as a temporal ellipsis.

21. Tschumi, *The Manhattan Transcripts*, 12.

22. To strengthen my hypothesis, I recall a passage from Derrida's archives at the IMEC: J. Derrida, "Deconstruction Philosophie, Deconstruction Architecture." Referring to "No (Point of) Madness—Maintaining Architecture," Derrida notes that: "In this text I attempted to account for what I perceived in Tschumi's work. Two things: on the one hand, his interest in the non-architectural models of architecture—he is interested in cinematographic narration, in a certain cinematographic time, in what takes place in time as time, in what opens up the architectural space to experience, not only the

experience of the spectator and of the inhabitant but also that of the visitor, of the one who performs the architectural space entering it, following a path, treating architecture not as a monumental building but as an experience that takes time and becomes evenemential in itself. But this model was not architectural, it comes from somewhere else. Indeed, there was a style characterized by a taste for disjunction, dissociation and separation. How does one build x so that the element of this construction remains dissociated and does not present as a beautiful, harmonious totality? So that this construction guards this species of respiration of discontinuity? (. . .) We have architecture when its disjointed elements are joined according to a modality of being together which is neither that of the system nor that of the synthesis, but the junction of the disjoined."

23. Cf. Tschumi, *The Manhattan Transcripts*, xix: "In architecture concepts can either precede or follow project or buildings. In other words, a theoretical concept may be either applied to a project or derived from it."

24. Derrida, "No (Point of) Madness—Maintaining Architecture," 96.

Chapter 6. Divergent Traces

1. W. J. Lillyman, M. F. Moriarty, and D. J. Neuman (eds.), *Critical Architecture and Contemporary Culture* (New York/Oxford: Oxford University Press, 1994).

2. W. Benjamin, "Experience and Poverty," in W. Benjamin, *Selected Writings: Volume 2 (1927–1934)*, trans. R. Livingstone et al. (Cambridge/London: Harvard University Press, 1999), 732: "Barbarism? Yes, indeed. We say this in order to introduce a new, positive concept of barbarism. For what does poverty of experience do for the barbarian? It forces him to start from scratch; to make a new start; to make a little go a long way; to begin with a little and build up further, looking neither left nor right. Among the great creative spirits, there have always been

the inexorable ones who begin by clearing a tabula rasa. They need a drawing table; they were constructors. . . . And this same insistence on starting from the very beginning also marks artists when they followed the example of mathematicians and built the world from stereometric forms, like the Cubist, or modeled themselves on engineers, like Klee. . . . A complex artist like the painter Paul Klee and a programmatic one like Loos—both reject the traditional, solemn, noble image of man, festooned with all the sacrificial offerings of the past. They turn instead to the naked man of the contemporary world who lies screaming like a newborn babe in the dirty diapers of the present."

3. J. Derrida, "Letter to Peter Eisenman," in Lillyman, Moriarty, and Neuman (eds.), *Critical Architecture and Contemporary Culture*, 20.

4. Ibid., 28.

5. J. Derrida, *Speech and Phenomena*, trans. D. B. Allison (Evanston: Northwestern University Press, 1973), 85. On Derrida's trace, see Gasché, *The Tain of the Mirror*, 186–194, in particular, 191: "As an originary nonpresence and alterity at the root of what Husserl conceptualized under the name *expression*—the ideal self-presence of meaning without the mediation of signs—the arche-trace is thought as the condition of the ideality of meaning and of self-presence in general, insofar as both must be infinitely repeatable in order to be what they are supposed to be. This necessary possibility of re-petition in its most general form—without which the ideality of meaning or self-presence, that is, of the domain proper of phenomenological investigation, could not come about—is 'the trace in the most universal sense.'. . . The originary trace is thus the constituting impurity or alterity, the constituting nonpresence, that allows the phenomenologically primordial to come into its own by providing the phenomenologically primordial with the mark of a minimal difference within which it can repeat itself infinitely as the same by referring to an Other and to (an Other of) itself within itself. In short, the arche-trace must be understood as the fold of an irreducible 'bending-back,' as a

minimal (self-difference) within (self-identity), which secures selfhood and self-presence through the detour of oneself (as Other) to oneself."

6. P. Eisenman, "Post/El Cards: A Reply to Jacques Derrida," in Lillyman, Moriarty, and Neuman (eds.), *Critical Architecture and Contemporary Culture*, 38.
7. Ibid., 40.
8. Ibid., 41.
9. Ibid.
10. Ibid., 42.
11. W. Benjamin, *The Work of Art in the Age of Its Technological Reproducibility, and Other Writings on Media*, trans. E. Jephcott et al. (Cambridge/London: Harvard University Press, 2008), 24.
12. Kipnis and Leeser, *Chora L Works*, 8.
13. Ibid., 9.
14. Ibid., 133–134.
15. P. Eisenman, "Moving Arrows, Eros, and Other Errors," in G. Vergani, P. Shinoda, and D. Kesler (eds.), *Precis: The Journal of the Columbia University Graduate School of Architecture, Planning and Preservation* 6, *The Culture of Fragments* (1987): 141.
16. Ibid., 142.
17. Ibid. Geoffrey Bennington, in an essay first published in 1986, had already revealed the inconsistency of Eisenman's discourse devoted to this project and more broadly as regards the question of "presentness." Cf. G. Bennington, "The Rationality of Postmodern Relativity," in G. Bennington, *Legislations: The Politics of Deconstruction* (London/New York: Verso, 1994), 190: "Eisenman's own presentations are also quite obscure and uneven. In the Romeo and Juliet material, for example, the attempt to disrupt the value of presence by opposing it to void and by redefining absence, is potentially confusing: and that re-definition of absence as 'either the trace of a previous presence' (in which case it 'contains memory'), or else as 'the trace of a possible presence' (in which case it 'contains immanence') could be shown to fall short of the Derridean account of the trace on which it is clearly attempting to draw: this account is essentially

that of a phenomenology such as is traversed by Derrida in *Of Grammatology* and *Speech and Phenomena*. By thinking in terms of memory and past or future presences, Eisenman is still within the metaphysical and essentially linear account of time which Derrida has so patiently undermined. It is also noticeable that Eisenman is still thinking in a fundamentally dialectical way, both in this account of absence and the temporality of the site, and in the three 'structural relationships' he takes from the story of Romeo and Juliet (the dialectic, of division, union, and then union-and-division of the lovers in the tomb). Derrida's own discussion of Romeo and Juliet (which there is no reason to assume that Eisenman would or should have known) disrupts this simplicity with a non-dialectical complexity, in which 'division' inhabits union as a non-accidental 'accident,' and division inhabits identity in, for example, the simultaneous unity and division of Romeo and his name."

18. However, some mitigating circumstances may be granted to Eisenman. He misunderstood deconstruction precisely because of deconstruction, that is, of an interpretation of deconstruction that was dominant at his time and derived from literary theory, the interpretation developed by Jonathan Culler in *On Deconstruction*. Eisenman knew this text quite well and he quoted it, in particular, in P. Eisenman, "The End of the Classical: The End of the Beginning, the End of the End," *Perspecta* 21 (1984). He does not mention the text in "Moving Arrows, Eros and Other Errors"; however, the description of the example of the arrow (Zenon's paradox) seems to derive precisely from *On Deconstruction*. Cf. J. Culler, *On Deconstruction: Theory and Criticism after Structuralism* (Ithaca: Cornell University Press, 1982), 94: "The metaphysics of presence is pervasive, familiar, and powerful. There is, however, a problem that it characteristically encounters: when arguments cite particular instances of presence as ground for further development, these instances invariably prove to be already complex constructions. What is proposed as a given, an elementary constituent, proves to be a product, dependent or derived in ways that deprive it of

the authority of simple or pure presence. Consider, for example, the flight of an arrow. If reality is what is present at any given instant, the arrow produces a paradox. At any given moment it is in a particular spot, it is always in a particular spot and never in motion. We want to insist, quite justifiably, that the arrow is in motion at every instant from the beginning to the end of its flight, yet its motion is never present at any moment of presence. *The presence of motion is conceivable, it turns out, only insofar as every instant is already marked with the traces of the past and of the future* [my emphasis]. Motion can be present, that is to say, only if the present instant is not something given but a product of the relations between past and future."

Chapter 7. Spacing

1. Cf. Vergani, Shinoda, and Kesler (eds.), *Precis: The Journal of the Columbia University Graduate School of Architecture, Planning and Preservation* 6, *The Culture of Fragments* (1987): 48–49.
2. Ibid., 7.
3. G. Vergani, P. Shinoda, D. Kesler, "Fragments of a Conversation with Jacques Derrida," *Precis: The Journal of the Columbia University Graduate School of Architecture, Planning and Preservation* 6 *The Culture of Fragments* (1987).
4. Ibid., 49.
5. Derrida, *Of Grammatology*, 158.
6. Vergani, Shinoda, and Kesler, "Fragments of a Conversation with Jacques Derrida," 49.
7. Derrida, *Glas*, 262.
8. Cf. J. Derrida, "*Ja*, or the *faux-bond*," in J. Derrida, *Points . . . Interviews, 1974–1994*, trans. P. Kamuf et al. (Stanford: Stanford University Press, 1995), 51–52: "Some have said that the last words left hanging ('. . . pour avoir compté sans' or in the other band, '. . . ici, maintenant, le débris de' {'. . . for it counted without' '. . . here, now, the debris of'}) because they seemed to pick up again the 'first' phrases of the book, formed a

Moebius strip. No, not at all: a caesura or hiatus prevents what in effect resembles such a band or strip from turning back on itself. The Moebius strip is a powerful figuration of the economy, of the law of reappropriation, or of successful mourning-work that can no longer, in the writing of *Glas* toll a knell {*sonner un glas*} which is its own (its *glas*) without breakage and debris. The *debris* of this band is not even the last or the first; it repeats and scatters the debris of a *bris de verre* {glass breakage} or of a mirror {glace}, and it has a multiple occurrence in the book . . . in short, before closing the book on a prefabricated Moebius strip, one has perhaps to let oneself be taken in a little longer by the words, the morsels of words or of dead bits in decomposition that let the writing go a bit more unbridled. And first of all with the word *débridé*. The Moebius strip is a detachable part in this treatise on detachment, an effect of partial simulacrum, a dead bit there where there is always more than one."

9. Derrida, *Of Grammatology*, 18.
10. Derrida, *Margins of Philosophy*, 10.
11. Derrida, *Of Grammatology*, 86.
12. Ibid.
13. Ibid., 86.
14. J. Derrida, "Prière d'insérer," in J. Derrida, *Glas*. This text is not present in the English edition. I thank Geoffrey Bennington for its translation.
15. Derrida, *Glas*, 75.
16. Ibid., 130.
17. Ibid., 116.
18. Ibid., 106.
19. Ibid., 72.
20. Ibid., 110.
21. Ibid., 79.
22. J. Derrida, "Proverb: 'He that would pun . . . ,'" in J. P. Leavey Jr., *Glassary* (Lincoln: University of Nebraska Press 1986), 17.

BIBLIOGRAPHY

Aristotle. *The Complete Works of Aristotle*. Ed. Jonathan Barnes. Princeton: Princeton University Press, vol. 2, 1991.

Benjamin, Walter. "Experience and Poverty." In W. Benjamin, *Selected Writings: Volume 2 (1927–1934)*. Trans. R. Livingstone et al. Cambridge/London: Harvard University Press, 1999.

———. *The Work of Art in the Age of Its Technological Reproducibility, and Other Writings on Media*. Trans. E. Jephcott et al. Cambridge/London: Harvard University Press, 2008.

Bennington, Geoffrey. "Derridabase." In G. Bennington and J. Derrida, *Derrida*, trans. G. Bennington. Chicago: University of Chicago Press, 1993.

——. "The Rationality of Postmodern Relativity." In G. Bennington, *Legislations: the Politics of Deconstruction*, London/New York: Verso, 1994.

Benveniste, Émile. *Le Vocabulaire des institutions indo-européennes. I. Économie, parenté, société*. Paris: Minuit, 1969.

Carpenter, Rhys. *The Architects of the Parthenon*. Harmondsworth: Penguin Books, 1970.

Culler, Jonathan. *On Deconstruction: Theory and Criticism after Structuralism*. Ithaca: Cornell University Press, 1982.

Derrida, Jacques. "Deconstruction Philosophie, Deconstruction Architecture." Unpublished seminar, IMEC Archives, Fond Derrida, 1996, DRR 192.

———. *Edmund Husserl's Origin of Geometry. An Introduction.* Trans. John P. Leavey Jr. Lincoln: University of Nebraska Press, 1989.

———. "Faith and Knowledge: The Two Sources of 'Religion' at the Limits of Reason Alone," trans. Samuel Weber. In J. Derrida and G. Vattimo (eds.), *Religion.* Stanford: Stanford University Press, 1998.

———. "Faxtexture." In C. C. Davidson (ed.), *Anywhere.* New York: Rizzoli, 1992.

———. "Fifty-Two Aphorisms for a Foreword." In J. Derrida, *Psyche: Inventions of the Other, Volume II*, ed. P. Kamuf and E. Rottenberg. Stanford: Stanford University Press, 2008.

———. "Générations d'une ville: mémoire, prophétie, responsabilité." In Alena Novotná Galard and Petr Kratochvíl (eds.), *Prague: Avenir d'une ville historique capitale.* Paris: L'Aube, 1992.

———. *Glas.* Trans. J. P. Leavey Jr. and R. Rand. Lincoln/London: University of Nebraska Press, 1986.

———. "Hospitality." *Angelaki: Journal of the Theoretical Humanitie* 3.5 (December 2000).

———. "Hospitality." In J. Derrida, *Acts of Religion*, ed. G. Anidjar. New York/London: Routledge, 2002.

———. "*Ja*, or the *faux-bond*." In J. Derrida, *Points . . . Interviews, 1974–1994*, trans. P. Kamuf et al. Stanford: Stanford University Press, 1995.

———. "Khōra." In J. Derrida, *On the Name*, trans. I. McLeod. Stanford: Stanford University Press, 1995. It was first published in J. Kipnis and T. Leeser (eds.), *Chora L Works: Jacques Derrida and Peter Eisenman.* New York: Monacelli Press, 1997; 1st ed. London: Architectural Association, 1991.

———. "Letter to Peter Eisenman." In W. J. Lillyman, M. F. Moriarty, and D. J. Neuman (eds.), *Critical Architecture and Contemporary Culture.* New York/Oxford: Oxford University Press, 1994.

———. "Nationalité et nationalisme philosophique: mythos, logos, topos." Unpublished seminar, Archive Derrida, IMEC, Caen, 1985/1986.

———. *Of Grammatology*. Trans. G. C. Spivak. Baltimore/London: Johns Hopkins University Press, 1976.

———. "On between the Lines." In D. Libeskind, *Radix-Matrix*. Munich/New York: Prestel, 1997.

———. *The Other Heading*: *Reflections on Today's Europe*. Trans. P.-A. Brault and M. Naas. Bloomington: Indiana University Press, 1992.

———. "The Pit and the Pyramid: Introduction to Hegel's Semiology." In J. Derrida, *Margins of Philosophy*, trans. A. Bass. Brighton: The Harvester Press, 1982.

———. "Plato's Pharmacy." In J. Derrida, *Dissémination*, trans. B. Johnson. London: The Athlone Press, 1981.

———. "Point de folies—Maintenant l'architecture." In B. Tschumi, *La case vide*: *La Villette*. London: Architectural Association, 1986; parallel English version published in J. Derrida, *Psyche*: *Inventions of the Other, Volume II*, as "No (Point of) Madness—Maintaining Architecture."

———. *The Politics of Friendship*. Trans. G. Collins. London/New York: Verso, 2005.

———. "Proverb: 'He that would pun . . . .'" In J. P. Leavey Jr., *Glassary*. Lincoln: University of Nebraska Press, 1986.

———. *Rogues*: *Two Essays on Reason*. Trans. P.-A. Brault and M. Naas. Stanford: Stanford University Press, 2005.

———. "Some Statements and Truisms about Neologism, Newisms, Postisms, Parasitisms and Other Small Seismisms." In D. Carrol (ed.), *The State of "Theory"*: *History, Art and Critical Discourse*. New York: Columbia University Press, 1990.

———. *Specters of Marx*. *The State of the Debt, the Work of Mourning and the New International*. Trans. P. Kamuf. New York/London: Routledge, 1994.

———. *Speech and Phenomena*. Trans. David B. Allison. Evanston: Northwestern University Press, 1973.

———. "Summary of Impromptu Remarks." In C. C. Davidson and J. Kipnis (eds.), *Anyone*. New York: Rizzoli, 1991.

———. "The Word Processor." In J. Derrida, *Paper Machine*, trans. R. Bowlby. Stanford: Stanford University Press, 2005.

Derrida, Jacques, Peter Brunette, and David Wills. "The Spatial Arts: An Interview with Jacques Derrida." In P. Brunette and D. Wills (eds.), *Deconstruction and the Visual Arts: Art, Media, Architecture*. Cambridge: Cambridge University Press, 1994.

Derrida, Jacques, and Anne Dufourmantelle. *Of Hospitality*. Trans. R. Bowlby. Stanford: Stanford University Press, 2000.

Derrida, Jacques, and Peter Eisenman. "Talking about Writing." *Any* 0 (March–May 1993).

Derrida, Jacques, Kurt Foster, and Wim Wenders. "The Berlin City Forum." *Architectural Design* 26.11/12 (1992): 46–53.

Derrida, Jacques, and Eva Mayer. "Labirinth und Architextur." In Vittorio Magnago Lampugnani (ed.), *Der Abenteuer den Ideen: Architektur und Philosophie seit industriellen Revolution*. Berlin: Staatliche Museen, National Galerie, 1984.

Derrida, Jacques, Bernard Tschumi, and Mark Wigley. "Invitation to Discussion." *Columbia Documents of Architecture and Theory* 1 (1992).

Eisenman, Peter. "The End of the Classical: The End of the Beginning, the End of the End." *Perspecta* 21 (1984).

———. "Moving Arrows, Eros, and Other Errors." In Gianmarco Vergani, Peter Shinoda, and David Kesler (eds.), *Precis: The Journal of the Columbia University Graduate School of Architecture, Planning and Preservation* 6, *The Culture of Fragments* (1987).

———. "Post/El Cards: A Reply to Jacques Derrida," in William J. Lillyman, Marilyn F. Moriarty and David J. Neuman (Eds.), *Critical architecture and Contemporary Culture*.

Gasché, Rodolphe. *The Tain of the Mirror: Derrida and the Philosophy of Reflection*. Cambridge/London: Harvard University Press, 1986.

———. *Views and Interviews: On "Deconstruction" in America*. Aurora: The Davies Group, 2007.

Heidegger, Martin. *Introduction to Metaphysics*. Trans. G. Fried and R. Polt. New Haven/London: Yale University Press, 2000.

Herodotus. *The Histories*. Trans. A. D. Godley. Cambridge: Harvard University Press, 1920.

Johnson, Philip, and Mark Wigley (eds.). *Deconstructivist Architecture*. New York: The Museum of Modern Art, 1988.

Leroi-Gourhan, André. *Gesture and Speech*. Trans. A. Bostock Berger. Cambridge/London: MIT Press, 1993.

Lillyman, William J., Marilyn F. Moriarty, and David J. Neuman (eds.). *Critical Architecture and Contemporary Culture*. New York/Oxford: Oxford University Press, 1994.

Kafka, Franz. "The City Coat of Arms." In F. Kafka, *The Great Wall of China: Stories and Reflections*. New York: Schocken Books, 1946.

Kipnis, Jeffrey, and Thomas Leeser (eds.). *Chora L Works: Jacques Derrida and Peter Eisenman*. New York: Monacelli Press, 1997; 1st ed. London: Architectural Association, 1991.

Mallet, Marie-Louise (ed.). *La Démocratie à venir: Autour de Jacques Derrida*. Paris: Galilée, 2004.

Martin, Luis. "Transpositions: On the Intellectual Origins of Tschumi's Architectural Theory." *Assemblage* 11 (1990).

Naas, Michael. *Miracle and Machine: Jacques Derrida and the Two Sources of Religion, Science, and the Media*. New York: Fordham University Press, 2012.

Pallasmaa, Juhani. *The Eyes of the Skin: Architecture and the Senses*. Chichester: Wiley & Sons, 2005.

Plato. *Complete Works*. Ed. John M. Cooper. Indianapolis/Cambridge: Hackett, 1997.

de Polignac, François. *Cults, Territory, and the Origins of the Greek City-State*. Trans. J. Lloyd. Chicago: University of Chicago Press, 1995.

Rykwert, Joseph. *The Idea of a Town*. Cambridge: MIT Press, 1988.

Sallis, John. *Chorology: On Beginning in Plato's Timaeus*. Bloomington/Indianapolis: Indiana University Press, 1999.

Sophocles. *Antigone*. Trans. R. Gibbons and C. Segal. Oxford: Oxford University Press, 2003.

Thucydides. *The Peloponnesian War*. Trans. R. Crawley. New York: Random House, 1951.

Tschumi, Bernard. *The Manhattan Transcripts*. London: Architectural Design, 1984; 2nd ed. St. Martin's Press/Academy Edition, 1995.

Vergani, Gianmarco, Peter Shinoda, and David Kesler. "Fragments of a Conversation with Jacques Derrida." *Precis: The Journal of the Columbia University Graduate School of Architecture, Planning and Preservation* 6 *The Culture of Fragments* (1987): 48–49.

Vernant, Jean-Pierre. "Hestia-Ermès: The Religious Expression of Space and Movement in Ancient Greece." In J.-P. Vernant, *Myth and Thought among the Greeks*. New York: Zone Books, 2006.

———. *Mythe et Religion en Grèce ancienne*. In J.-P. Vernant, *Œuvres*, vol. 1: *Religions, rationalités, politique*. Paris: Seuil, 2007.

———. *The Origins of Greek Thought*. Ithaca: Cornell University Press, 1982.

Vidler, Anthony. *The Architectural Uncanny: Essays in the Modern Unhomely*. Cambridge/London: MIT Press, 1992.

———. "The Explosion of Space: Architecture and the Filmic Imaginary." *Assemblage* 21 (1993).

———. "Nothing to Do with Architecture." *Gray Room* 21 (Fall 2005): 112–127.

Wigley, Mark. *The Architecture of Deconstruction: Derrida's Haunt*. London/Cambridge: MIT Press, 1993.

Wittgenstein, Ludwig. *Tractatus Logico-Philosophicus*. Trans. D. F. Pears and B. F. McGuinness. London/New York: Routledge, 2001.

Xenophon. *Memorabilia*. Trans. A. L. Bonnette. Ithaca: Cornell University Press, 1994.Aristotle, 4, 104, 122n5

NAME INDEX

Benjamin, Walter, 79, 80, 86, 90, 91, 131n2, 133n11
Bennington, Geoffrey, 112n13, 133n17, 136n14
Benveniste, Emile, 122n13
Brunette, Peter, 33, 34

Carpenter, Rhys, 121n11
Cimon, 7, 24
Coop Himmelb(l)au, x
Culler, Jonathan, 134n18

Davidson, Cinthia C., ix

Eisenman, Peter, vii, ix, x, xvi, xvii, xix, 3, 6, 17, 22, 49, 79, 80–97, 111n2, 112n11, 113n17, 133n6, 133n15, 133n17, 134n17

Gasché, Rodolphe, 112n13, 125n2, 132n5
Gehry, Frank, x
Genet, Jean, 100, 106–109.

Hadid, Zaha, x
Hegel, Georg, Wilhelm, Friedrich, 48, 52, 53, 54, 90, 98, 99, 100, 104–110

Heidegger, Martin, xiii, xv, xvii, 4, 18, 82, 92, 104, 119n3
Herodotus, 120n9
Husserl, Edmund, 55, 83, 84, 132n5

Johnson, Philip, 112n11, 129n12

Leroi-Gourhan, André, 59, 65, 104, 127n19, 129n3
Libeskind, Daniel, x

Kafka, Franz, 39, 124n24
Kipnis, Geffrey, vii, ix, 133n8
Koolhaas, Rem, x

Martin, Luis, 130n17

Naas, Michael, 123n6

Pallasmaa, Juhani, 130n16
Pericles, 7, 23, 24, 25, 116n13
Plato, xv, 3, 4, 5, 8, 14, 17, 25, 28, 31, 52, 54, 56, 63, 83, 101, 113n17, 116n13
De Polignac, François, 119n8

Rykwert, Joseph, 21, 119n6, 119n7

Sallis, John, 118n23
Saussure, Ferdinand, 52, 56, 83, 100–104
Sophocles, 54, 126n10

Thucydides, 121n10, 122n13
Tschumi, Bernard, vii, viii, ix, x, xix, 27, 46, 61, 62, 63, 66–78, 92, 111n6, 111n12, 13, 113n17, 129n14, 130n17, 130n22, 131n23

Vernant, Jean-Pierre, 19, 21, 22, 117n13, 119n5, 119n7, 121n12, 123n9, 124n9
Vidler, Anthony, ix, 113n17, 116n6, 118n26, 129n12, 130n19

Wenders, Wim, 38
Wigley, Marc, ix, 111n6, 112n11, 113–115n17, 129n12
Wills, David, 33
Wittgenstein, Ludwig, 129n14

www.ingramcontent.com/pod-product-compliance
Lightning Source LLC
Chambersburg PA
CBHW030828230426
43667CB00008B/1425